Manzanar to Mount Whitney

Manzanar to Mount Whitney

The Life and Times of a Lost Hiker

Hank Umemoto

Heyday, Berkeley, California

This project was made possible in part by a generous grant from the California Civil Liberties Public Education Program.

Library of Congress Cataloging-in-Publication Data

Umemoto, Hank.
 Manzanar to Mount Whitney : the life and times of a lost hiker / Hank Umemoto.
    p. cm.
 ISBN 978-1-59714-202-1 (pbk. : alk. paper)
1. Umemoto, Hank. 2. Japanese Americans--California--Biography. 3. Japanese Americans--Evacuation and relocation, 1942-1945. 4. Manzanar War Relocation Center. 5. Korean War, 1950-1953--Personal narratives, American. 6. Businesspeople--California--Biography. 7. Mountaineering--California--Whitney, Mount. I. Title.
F870.J3U44 2012
940.53'1779487092--dc23
 [B]
                        2012023947

Book Design: Lorraine Rath
Printed in La Vergne, TN, by Lightning Source Inc.

Orders, inquiries, and correspondence should be addressed to:
Heyday
P.O. Box 9145, Berkeley, CA 94709
(510) 549-3564, Fax (510) 549-1889
www.heydaybooks.com

10   9   8   7   6   5   4   3   2

In memory of Ryosuke and Kusu Umemoto
and
Torakichi Muro

Contents

Prologue

On August 10, 1988, President Ronald Reagan signed the Civil Liberties Act of 1988, which authorized the payment of $20,000 of restitution to eligible Japanese Americans who had been unjustly interned in the United States during World War II. The act also included an apology, the creation of a public education fund, and redress for Aleutians who had been held in temporary camps in southeast Alaska.

According to the act, the U.S. Attorney's Office was responsible for locating eligible individuals through government records and a public awareness campaign.

From January 1991 to February 1993, Hank Shozo Umemoto received four form letters from the U.S. Department of Justice's Office of Redress Administration requesting documents to verify his case for redress payment.

Up to that time, he had never responded.

Then, finally, in a letter dated February 5, 1993, Hank Umemoto officially refused monetary restitution.

U.S. Department of Justice
Civil Rights Division
Office of Redress Administration
Verification Unit
Washington, D.C.

February 23, 1993

Dear Mr. Umemoto:

This is in response to your letter dated February 5, 1993, regarding the Office of Redress Administration's (ORA) determination that you are potentially eligible for a redress payment pursuant to Section 105 of the Civil Liberties Act of 1988. In your letter, you stated that you elected to refuse the $20,000 redress payment to which you may be entitled.

In accordance with 28 CFR Part 74.11 of the regulations implementing the Act, your record of written refusal has been filed with ORA and the amount shall remain in the Civil Liberties Public Education Fund.

Your refusal constitutes the final action in your case, and no payment may be made hereafter to you or your heirs.

Sincerely,

Paul W. Suddes (Signed)
Administrator for Redress

Introduction

"Fuck you!" I yelled, followed by a one-finger gesture.

The driver brought his jeep to a quick halt, got out, and walked toward me. His fellow soldier, riding shotgun, followed with a rifle under his arm.

"What did you say?" the driver asked. His partner inched forward until he had me looking up the barrel of his rifle. I was terrified and trembling with fear.

"Nnnn…nothing," I stuttered and lied.

Just a few weeks earlier, I was a thirteen-year-old seventh-grader at Sierra School in Florin, located in the San Joaquin Valley of California. During the latter part of May 1942, six months after Pearl Harbor, our family bid farewell to the farm where my immigrant parents had toiled for over thirty years.

We were ordered to report to the Elk Grove railroad depot, where a train would take us to Manzanar. Grasping onto my duffel bag, I boarded the train, following the directions of armed soldiers. As night approached, we were ordered to lower our shades and were forbidden to peek outside, but when the train began to lose speed on an incline over Tehachapi Pass, I could not resist the temptation of finding out what was happening.

I pulled back the shade and laid eyes on the most spectacular sight I had ever seen. Silhouettes of pine trees against the Milky Way were casting shadows in the moonlight. It was a breathtaking image forever imprinted on my mind, and although I felt deserted and lonely, I also experienced something warm, peaceful, and serene.

"Close the shade." I heard a voice and felt someone tapping on my shoulder. Stunned, I looked back and saw a soldier holding a rifle in one hand with its butt resting on the floor. I immediately complied with his demand. In this moment, I realized that being denied the right to enjoy the wonderful creations of God, I was no longer a free man in a land where every person is endowed with equal privileges. I was just another prisoner.

By sunrise, we were transferred to a Santa Fe Trailways bus at the desert town of Mojave, to be driven from there to a location called Manzanar. The now-dry Owens Lake was then filled with saline water, and on its surface the morning sun cast a white and blue reflection against the backdrop of the rust-colored Inyo Mountains. To the west I saw the majestic Mount Williamson, and the Sierra Nevada Range, capped with snow, disappeared into the northern horizon. It was unbelievable that we would be living in such beautiful and scenic splendor.

It was 10 a.m. when the bus stopped next to the Block 30 mess hall. We walked from there in ankle-deep soft sand to Room 3 of Barrack 2, the tarpapered building my mother, my brother Ben, his wife Annie, their son Ronnie, my sister Edith, and I were to call our new home.

The scenery was magnificent and the air was crisp; it was a perfect spring morning. In early afternoon, however, the strong northerly wind began to surface, bringing the loose sand and dust through gaps in the windows and cracks in the wooden floor. It became a dust storm of near-suffocating magnitude. At suppertime, after standing in line for what felt like forever, I entered the mess hall, and to my surprise and elation I saw my friend Frank, whom I joined at his table with a plateful of stew and mashed potatoes. By sundown, the dust storm had subsided and a gentle breeze infiltrated the late-spring evening.

I visited Frank the following morning, and while we were sitting on his doorstep, the jeep passed by. Enclosed by barbed wire, monitored by soldiers in the towers along its parameters, and with two armed soldiers patrolling in the jeep, I again wondered if the "land of the free" we sang about in the classroom was nothing but a farce.

It was then that I yelled out, voicing my feelings with profanity and accompanying my words with that discourteous salute to the soldiers in the jeep.

In retrospect, I'm glad I had expressed myself, but I'm also ashamed I had acted like a coward and lied to the soldiers, saying I had blurted out nothing.

It was ten o'clock, exactly twenty-four hours since setting foot on the sandy loam of Manzanar that I called my home for the next three years. With each passing day, a metamorphosis was taking effect, gradually shedding the aggression, the hostility, and the mixed-up emotions of a mixed-up teenager.

◆ ◆ ◆

One evening some months later, the crimson sky over the Sierra had turned to deep indigo and the stars had begun to sprinkle the eastern horizon. It was time to call it a day and return to our barracks. Through the window, two eerie, faint flickering lights appeared and descended the mountain, sending shivers down my spine.

I described this incident to Frank as we walked to school the following morning.

"Yeah, I saw that, too," he said. "That was two hikers with flashlights coming down from Whitney Portal."

"Whitney Portal? What's that?" It sounded to me like a port-hole on a ship, and I was confused.

"Well, that's where you can drive up and park your car. From there, you can start hiking to reach the top of Mount Whitney."

"You mean we could climb to the top?" I was curious and anxious to think that perhaps we could climb it, too.

"Not *we*, you asshole! You gotta be a free man to climb it."

In that moment, I made a vow to climb Mount Whitney someday. I had no idea, however, that this trek would take me so long.

Chapter One

ICEHOUSE CANYON

My friend and I were reminiscing about the good ole days at Manzanar one evening when one of my children asked, "Where's Manzanar?"

"Well, Manzanar is..." I hesitated for a moment, trying to relate the camp to some well-known landmark. Saying that it is located in Owens Valley or near Lone Pine would be meaningless. Finally, I said, "Manzanar is close to Mount Whitney," since everyone knows Mount Whitney. As an afterthought I added, "You could even hike it from Manzanar."

"Can we hike Mount Whitney?" the rest of my children joined in.

"Yeah, we'll all hike Mount Whitney together when you kids are a little older."

Not only had I made a vow to climb the Big One, now I had committed myself to taking all four kids up Mount Whitney someday.

Kids grow like weeds, though, and soon enough they were on their separate ways, with absolutely no interest in spending time with their parents. I felt safe to assume they had forgotten about climbing Mount Whitney. I was relieved that the commitment I had made several decades ago was something I no longer had to honor.

When my lifelong friend underwent triple bypass surgery, my oldest daughter, Karen, asked, "How's your health, Dad?"

"Great! I could out-hike any of you kids!" I boasted. I meant it as a joke, since it was ludicrous that this sixty-seven-year-old man could seriously challenge his thirty-seven-year-old daughter.

"Okay. How about some Saturday?"

"Sure. Sounds great. Just let me know the time and the place." I went along with the joke, since nobody would ever take my challenge seriously. And yet, days later, an email message from Karen flashed on the screen: "How about Icehouse Canyon Trail this Saturday morning at eight?"

This was totally unexpected, and I initially perceived it as a continuation of our joke, but without a "ha ha" or some other note to that effect, I concluded that she was indeed serious, and I reluctantly agreed to meet her at the trailhead.

I arrived at an asphalt parking lot at the head of Icehouse Canyon Trail two hours early. Icehouse Canyon is a mile and a half past Mount Baldy Village in the eastern San Gabriel Mountains north of Los Angeles.

"I was here a couple hours early to acclimate to the altitude," I said when Karen and my son-in-law Brian arrived. I talked like a seasoned hiker, using the hikers' jargon I picked up on the Internet. I later regretted opening my chops when I found that talking the walk was easy but actually walking it was something else.

We had hiked up the moderate gradient of Icehouse Canyon Trail for a few hundred yards when the tendons surrounding my ankles became sore. Another short stretch over rugged terrain and my calves began to ache, followed by a throbbing heart and shortness of breath. Shortly thereafter, by the time we approached a fork in the trail, the situation had worsened with wobbly knees as well as a slight tightening of muscles in my thighs.

The trail to the right seemed rugged and steep, and attempting it was out of the question, but since the one to the left seemed much more inviting and easier, although a little longer, I suggested we take that route.

"The scenery seems a lot better on this longer trail," I remarked, although that was not a good reason, since I later discovered that the more strenuous trail was far more awe-inspiring. Besides, even on the milder trail, exhaustion overtook my body after two miles.

"Lunchtime," Karen suggested, probably noticing my strained breathing, slurred speech, and unstable footing. I probably looked like someone who'd had too many beers.

I sat on a nearby boulder with my bologna sandwich. My muscles began to tighten, and the tension in my thighs intensified and turned into painful cramps until all I could do was lie flat on my back and relax until the pain faded away. This was not the first time I had felt exhaustion like this.

* * *

In 1989, I bought a Winnebago motor home so we could enjoy our future retirement years. Together with our pet miniature Schnauzer, Chiko, we started on a trip to a campground on the eastern slope of the Sierra off Highway 395, south of Mono Lake. Veering off the highway, it was a bumpy, dusty ride to the remote camping area. My intent was to escape from people and civilization, and I assumed nobody else was foolish enough to come to such a primitive campground, whose only amenity was a portable outhouse with a liberal share of stench. To my surprise, there was another pair of campers at the site. I parked the RV near a young man in his mid-twenties who was fiddling with what looked like a walkie-talkie.

"He just got that CB radio and has been trying all morning to get some signals on it," his wife teased.

After settling in, Chiyoko decided to stay at camp while Chiko and I went for a walk. We proceeded up what seemed like a narrow foot trail leading to somewhere. Where, I hadn't the slightest clue. We soon reached a fire road that was wide enough for two cars to pass. The dirt pathway was built and maintained as an access road into the forest for firefighters and their equipment in case of a flare-up. Strolling along the road on a slight rise, we reached the end at what appeared to be a place where obsidian was being mined. It was the size of half a football field, with gigantic glistening onyx-like boulders covering every inch of the surface.

"I'll keep this as a good luck charm," I told Chiko as I picked up and pocketed a small, shiny piece of jet black stone.

We began to walk back to camp on the wide fire road. The trail turning off it to our camp was a narrow path almost completely hidden in the bushy terrain, hardly visible from the road. An experienced hiker would have placed a duck (a pile of stones) to designate the intersection, but being a novice hiker, I overlooked that detail. Without a visible clue showing where I should turn off into the trail back to the RV, I continued walking on the road, past the trailhead to our camp, constantly looking for the evasive footpath that was nowhere in sight.

Chiko was panting, and I was also feeling thirsty, since it had been several hours since we'd left our camp. Every hundred steps or so, I had to stop and lie flat on my back in the middle of the fire road, my arms and legs outstretched, as though asking some divine power to whisk me away from the misery. We were at 8,500 feet, and as I lay there I watched a large elongated puffy cloud pass so low overhead I imagined I could almost stroke it with my hands. "Heavenly" was the only word befitting the experience.

Meanwhile, back at the campground, Chiyoko had decided to join us on the walk and closed the RV door behind her. When she couldn't find us after a short search, she went back to the RV and tried to get inside, only to discover that it was locked. After a couple hours, with me and Chiko still on the trail, she became concerned and asked the camper with the CB radio to contact the Mono County Sheriff's Department.

A short while later, a deputy arrived. It was then he learned that Chiyoko, who had left Los Angeles as an infant and lived in Japan for the next twenty-five years, did not speak English. The deputy immediately radioed June Lake, a seasonal sports-fishing community, to see if there were any Nisei (second-generation Japanese American people) fishing at the loop, since one of the many stereotypes of the Nisei is that they are all fishermen.

Once, when I was fishing in the High Sierra, a fisherman approached me to ask about a night crawler. I didn't have the slightest inkling what a night crawler was, but I assumed it was some type of worm. The only worm I was familiar with were the ones I'd dug out of our vegetable garden before I went fishing at the nearby murky pond as a child, hoping to hook catfish and carp.

"Sorry, I'm new at this and don't know much about night crawlers," I replied. Although tempted, I dared not ask him "By the way, what's a night crawler?"

As it turns out, there was a Japanese-speaker at June Lake. The deputy left Chiyoko at the campground, drove about ten miles north, and brought back a Nisei woman in her mid-sixties to act as a translator. She was renting a cabin at June Lake for a fishing jaunt.

Meanwhile, trudging along the fire road with Chiko, I noticed that she was walking with a limp. I kneeled down and placed her on her back on my lap to examine her paws. They were bleeding.

"I'll just have to carry you," I said. Things weren't going too well, and it occurred to me that perhaps I was jinxed. I put my hand in my pocket, retrieved the shiny black good luck piece, fumbled with it for a while, and then hurled it as far as I could.

A faded vintage Ford pickup rambled up the road. The driver, on his way to collect firewood with his wife and seven-year-old son, stopped. It was obvious to them that I was totally lost and disoriented.

"I'm camped at a primitive campground," I told them. "Near those huge black rocks."

"You mean the Obsidian Dome. It's that way." He pointed in the opposite direction. "I think you were going the wrong way." He laughed.

His wife, taking pity on Chiko and me, left us with a fresh bottle of water. I immediately poured some in my palm and let Chiko lick it up. While we were satiating our thirst, the truck stopped again, made a U-turn, and drove toward us.

"Hop in the back," the driver said. "I'll take you to the camp." It turned out to be quite a long drive, and I realized I had been off course by a greater distance than I had imagined.

On our way to the campground, we encountered a white pickup with the National Forest insignia on its door.

"So you found him!" the ranger yelled out the window when he saw me in the back of the truck. He gave us a thumbs-up and drove on. As we approached the camp, I saw a Mono County Sheriff SUV and two large white vans, with eight men and two dogs gathered in a circle as though discussing some tactical rescue maneuver.

"We had a helicopter on standby," one fellow said, smiling. I couldn't tell whether he was serious or joking.

I didn't say a word. I was totally embarrassed that my stupidity had caused so much trouble to so many people. Among all the embarrassing moments of my life, the Obsidian Dome incident ranks at the top of the list.

* * *

Here I was again up a mountain, in the middle of a trail, while Karen and Brian finished their lunch.

"We'll scout around and see what's up ahead," Brian said nonchalantly, in an effort to preserve my pride and spare me from further embarrassment. I rested while they went up to the end of Icehouse Canyon Trail, where there is a level area called Icehouse Saddle, so called because it is shaped like a horse saddle with four hiking trails extending outward in different directions like tentacles of an octopus.

By the time they returned, my thigh cramps were bearable, and I was able to walk. Descending the mountain wasn't any easier, though, since it was then that I began to suffer a pain in my stomach. Midway down the mountain, Karen said something that I had always wished I would never hear.

"We still have to climb Mount Whitney." She had remembered the promise I'd made to the children many years ago.

Oh no! I thought. *I should have known better than to promise my kids anything because they'll remember until the day I die!*

I wished that I had climbed Mount Whitney earlier in my youth, when I was physically capable, but I had never had the financial means to travel to Whitney from Los Angeles. By the time I had a car and a few dollars to spare, the Korean War had erupted, and I was stationed on the other side of the world. The Mount Whitney trek was placed on the back burner. After returning from overseas, I was married, and *poof!* went the dream of climbing the Big One, along with other carefree bachelor cravings.

Now, decades later, climbing Mount Whitney was out of my mind, and the obligation of taking the kids up it had been just a spur-of-the-moment empty promise that I'd hoped nobody would ever expect to be honored.

"Absolutely! We'll all go up Whitney, all five of us!" I told Karen. Laughing on the inside, I remained poker-faced. Who in their right mind would expect an old man to tackle that hike? At 14,505 feet, Mount Whitney is the tallest peak in the contiguous forty-eight states. Each year thirty thousand hikers attempt to conquer it; only ten thousand make it to the top.

Meanwhile, my stomach pains had worsened, and the resurrection of the promise to climb Mount Whitney certainly didn't help the situation. I scurried to a secluded spot to squat.

"We'll have to start training for it," Karen warned after I joined them back on the trail.

"Of course!" I agreed, with a trace of sarcasm in my voice. I was exhausted, and as I walked to the car, I was out of breath, and everything below my hip was aching so much that I was convinced my hiking days were behind me.

But the following Saturday, I got up early. *I'll just humor them,* I thought, and I prepared to attempt Icehouse Canyon Trail again. To my astonishment, I made it to the Saddle. So the week after that I tried the more difficult trail. With each excursion, I was able to go a little farther. Unknowingly, I became hooked on the fresh mountain air and scenery.

At Icehouse Saddle, there is a trail leading north to Timber Mountain, at 8,500 feet. Having gained much confidence, I made an attempt to climb it but soon realized my confidence was misleading, since I found myself succumbing to exhaustion even with the summit in sight.

"How's it going?" A hiker passed by, briskly walking up to the summit as though he were taking a morning stroll in the park.

Just to say "Not so good" sapped all the energy out of me. A couple of minutes later, he was passing me going the opposite direction, waving goodbye as he sidestepped down the trail with ease.

With the top of Timber Mountain only few hundred yards away, I headed for the summit the only way I could: by taking a moment's rest after each move forward. One step at a time, I finally struggled to the top. I marked it as a successful day and returned home ready to hike again the following Saturday.

The following week, the challenge was Telegraph Peak, at 8,900 feet. Passing Timber Mountain, I stood on a ridge and studied the trail leading to Telegraph Peak. The trail went down hundreds of feet before leading up to the summit. *What if I don't have the stamina to hike uphill on the return trek?* I thought. I finally decided to chance it and continued on, relieved to realize later that my apprehension was just an overreaction. I returned from Telegraph Peak, stood at the Saddle, and looked south. *Ontario Peak is for next week,* I told myself. I scanned the mountains to the east. *Cucamonga Peak will be after that,* I pledged.

I sat back against a boulder. Among the several hikers resting at the Saddle before the next leg of their trek was an old man reclining against a fallen ponderosa pine. Leaning to the side, his legs outstretched, he wore a tilted red hat. A faded and worn backpack rested beside him. He was obviously a veteran hiker, someone who had traveled the mountain trails at least a thousand times. He seemed to be arriving at the end of his journey, weathered and hardened like the barkless tree behind him—tired but content, pursuing and absorbing the endless wonders of nature that surrounded him.

Maybe he lives in the mountains, I pondered, *or could he possibly be a derelict searching for his lost soul? At least one thing's certain...he's the oldest hiker I've ever seen on a mountain trail!*

He stood up then, and with a long aluminum cane he began his descent with a slow but well-coordinated gait. He was tall and nimble, and graceful in his strides.

When I caught up to him, I remarked, "I'm getting too old for this!"

"Hell, I'm seventy-eight," he said. He was neither overly talkative nor especially friendly. He had a frown on his face, as though he were reprimanding me for saying I was too old, at many years his junior. Observing his bristly attitude, I had a ridiculous thought: that this man was possibly a "Jap hater."

His name was Wilson, and little did I know at the time that he was later to become my hiking friend. We often tackled Mount Baldy together, and he nurtured my seemingly impossible fantasy of climbing Mount Whitney. I met him at the Mount Baldy summit one day and we sat and chatted for a while. He was eighty-two years old at the time, and that was the last time I ever saw him. I often looked for him, an old man with a tilted red hat, and I kept my ears tuned for the *click-clack* of his aluminum cane as he hiked up a rocky slope. He has been and will forever be my inspiration; old soldiers fade away, but an old, weary hiker keeps trudging to his journey's end, and to eternal bliss.

So it was there, at Icehouse Canyon, where I slowly became fond of—and addicted to—hiking the local mountains. It was there I was inspired to climb Mount Baldy and Mount San Gorgonio, two of the highest and most popular peaks in Southern California. It was also at Icehouse Canyon, during that fall I turned sixty-eight, that I developed a real hope of climbing Mount Whitney. Before that, it was just a crazy old man's dream, never expected to materialize.

Chapter Two

BARE HANDS, PURE GUTS, AND DETERMINATION

"Good morning!" I called out to an elderly woman standing in front of her cottage on a steep, narrow, winding forest road. She frowned, as if I didn't belong in her world. Well, I probably didn't. I was a Nisei man, completely lost in San Bernardino National Forest somewhere off of Highway 38.

"I've been looking for the trailhead to San Bernardino Mountain Peak," I told her out the driver's-side window. "Now I'm lost." Realizing that I was just a wandering hiker and no threat to her, she pointed back to where I had come from.

"Make a U-turn and then turn right on the main road and look for Camp Angelus Fire Station, Sonny. Then you'll see a sign."

Sonny? Hey, I'm sixty-eight! I thought. She must have been in her mid-eighties and I must have been just a child in her eyes. Or perhaps it was because I was driving a bright blue off-road truck with a large 4x4 decal on the door and fancy chrome wheels with oversized tires, rather unusual for a person my age.

I followed her directions and was soon on the trail to San Bernardino Peak. The hiking trail that carved through the forest was heavenly with lush green ground cover amid thriving pine trees. Then suddenly the trail descended, causing me to wonder if I were going in the wrong direction. The narrow trail eventually led to a campground with a small stream trickling through the area marked with fallen pine trees, boulders, and a carpet of green grass, making the place a staggering beauty. There was a large tree trunk broken off a few feet above the ground, a vision that could only be portrayed in an oil painting; the campground was in the image of Eden. It was secluded, with no sign of recent human visitation.

Hopping over the stream and taking a closer look to assess its potential as my future campsite, I realized why it was in such an undisturbed, virgin state. The entire area was swarming with large black ants, all over the ground and around the dead tree trunks. Just standing there for a few moments in the mirage of this disillusioned Garden of Eden was enough to send goose pimples over my body. It reminded me of the stories that Issei folks (first-generation Japanese immigrants) told us time and again of how they had perceived America as a land where "money grew on trees," as they often phrased it. For my parents and their peers, perhaps it was like hopping over a stream to a land that seemed to be filled with wealth and luxury, only to discover that it also contains hardship and disappointment.

* * *

Both my parents were immigrants from Japan and were like the early American pioneers: dreamers who arrived in this country with nothing but guts and determination to tame the wild frontier, survivors who saw Tomorrow as an obstacle to overcome.

Father, at nineteen, was living in a town called Minoshima in Wakayama Prefecture in Japan and had a girlfriend whom he was planning to marry, but one evening while calling on her, he accidentally saw her *tachi-shoben* (*tachi* means to stand, and *shoben* to urinate). Since this was 1889, it was considered unladylike for a woman to assume such a posture, and that was enough for Father to want to call off the engagement, although first he had to find a diplomatic and subtle approach of relating his intentions, rather than just saying, "Hey, let's call off the engagement because I don't like the way you urinate."

Shortly after that incident, he had an opportunity to go to Hokkaido. Taking advantage of this excuse to escape his commitment to be married, he departed with his friend to the untamed frontier, where they bought a piece of land to farm. Two years later, after the farm project proved a dismal failure, he boarded an ocean liner to San Francisco to seek greater prospects. Upon arriving in America, he settled in the San Joaquin Valley of California, working as a migrant farm laborer and saving money to start his own venture growing celery in the Salinas area with a partner. Celery was an ultra-high-risk crop; it could raise men from rags to riches overnight, or, in Father's case, turned him and his partner into rags in just a few short years.

My father sought a more secure venture, while his partner remained in celery farming, eventually becoming a millionaire in the business. Father, on the other hand, bought new land in a region about nine miles east of the state capital. It was a territory with colorful vistas as well as a vibrant history, starting with Nisenan Indian tribes who had once reigned there, calling it their home for hundreds of years before being pushed out by newcomers. Many forty-niners who had abandoned their hopes of striking it rich settled in this area, followed by cattlemen, who were awed at the fertility of this gently rolling landscape. They named this area, covered with wildflowers in the spring, Florin.

In late 1890, the first generation of Japanese immigrants began to trickle into Florin as strawberry farmers and grape growers. They were followed by a vast influx of Issei at the turn of the new century.

In 1910, at the age of thirty, Father purchased a twenty-acre parcel in the Florin area. The land was only a stone's throw from Mr. and Mrs. Iba, relatives of Father's. How they were related, I never found out; all I knew is that they were kinfolk. He stayed at the Ibas' until he had a well dug on his land for irrigation and a little shed for the two horses he had purchased from Tsumbo-*san* to cultivate the land. Tsumbo-*san* was a partially deaf Portuguese immigrant horse rancher who sold horses to Issei farmers in Florin and the surrounding agricultural region. Popular and well liked by the Issei, he was given the Japanese name Tsumbo-*san*—*tsumbo* meaning deaf (perhaps not extremely complimentary), but nevertheless followed by *san*, which is an address of respect and esteem.

Father started his vineyard by planting cuttings from discarded grape branches taken from the Ibas' vineyard after the pruning season. Next to the grapevines, he planted strawberries. By 1912, with a modest income, high hopes, and elevated dreams, he donned his black suit and a tie and visited a Japanese photographer in Sacramento. He slapped on a fake Wyatt Earp mustache and posed for a portrait. With a little touch-up, it became a picture of the handsomest of men. This photo accompanied a letter Father sent to his elder brother in Japan, to whom he bragged that he was the owner of over twelve hundred *tsubo* (twenty acres) of fertile land, an incredibly huge holding for a single individual by the Japanese standard. Father also requested a wife be sent to him.

Father's brother, who was operating the family wholesale farming equipment and supply business in Minoshima, had an important customer named Hiramatsu, who had sizeable land holdings himself. Mr. Hiramatsu also had a sizeable number of daughters. Father's brother acted as a *baishakunin* (go-between), and a proposal was made to Kusu, the remaining spinster among the eleven daughters, to become a picture bride to a farmer in America. Kusu promptly agreed, since it was the wish of her mother and also probably because one of her older sisters was married to Mr. Iwasaki, who lived in the Sacramento Delta region, only thirty miles from Florin.

Kusu arrived in San Francisco on the ocean liner *Chichibu-Maru* in 1912 and was ferried to Angel Island, in San Francisco Bay, for processing. Father stood on the pier at Angel Island with over a dozen other Issei grooms, each with a picture in hand, constantly shifting their eyes from their pictures to the girls strolling down the pier, attempting to find a match.

"Hiramatsu Kusu-*san*?" father asked the women who seemed to fit the profile in the photograph he held in his hand.

"*Hai.* Umemoto-*sama*?"

She was ashen and skinny, hardly the type my father had envisioned. He needed someone more robust to help develop his land, and during a moment of disillusionment a thought flashed through his mind that he should deport her back home to Japan. Mother's family, part of a samurai warrior lineage, owned a sake brewery in addition to their substantial land hold-ings, so the daughters grew up with several maids to do all their daily chores. Since mother—nicknamed Itohan by the workers because she often made clothes for them (*ito* means thread and *han* is a slang for -*san*)—had no physical duties, she was indeed frail, and considered absolutely useless in Father's eyes.

Will she survive the scorching hundred-degree heat in the summer and the freezing twenty-degree cold in the winter? How about digging ditches and picking strawberries and grapes, and lugging a fifty-pound crate all day long? These thoughts and many more passed through his mind as he welcomed her to this country. Unbeknownst to either of them at the time, my mother was also in the early stages of tuberculosis, an ailment diagnosed approximately forty years later when her doctor detected scar tissue the size of a dollar coin on her lung. The doctor said the disease had been cured naturally by the hot, dry air of the northern San Joaquin Valley. In that way, coming to America saved her life.

Mother, like other Issei picture brides I later met, never discussed how she felt about the arranged marriage or how a romance developed between two absolute strangers. Maybe it was a sacred part of their lives, to be honored and cherished only between husband and wife.

In time, Father abandoned the thought of deporting Mother to her homeland, since she was indeed a good wife and labored without complaining. Father also reconsidered my mother's appearance. He realized that she was pretty (except for her buck teeth), and perhaps not totally useless, as he had initially surmised. Thus began the life of Mr. and Mrs. Ryosuke Umemoto, husband and wife. Eventually, with dentures, even mother's buck teeth were not a problem.

For their honeymoon, they worked picking hops, a plant used as a bittering agent in beer. "*Hoppusu-tsumi*" (picking hops) mother used to say as we thumbed through her photo album years later. She often shared her memories of how they took the first fifty dollars they earned to buy lumber to build the first decent structure on their newly acquired land.

It was their honeymoon cottage, but with a dirt floor, it was definitely not luxurious. Still, Mother always said if she had to pick out a single best and most memorable time of her life, she certainly would have picked that first year of marriage, even though it was one of their most strenuous.

Mother and Father's strawberries and grapes were shipped to the eastern part of the country from Florin's railroad loading dock. To cater to the Issei farmers in the region, Japanese merchants established their business near the loading dock and also set up a market, a dry goods store, and a garage, as well as Japanese Methodist and Buddhist churches.

As the town of Florin began to prosper and grow, so did our family. Several years before World War I, my oldest brother, Ben, was born, followed by Sam three years later. After the war, sister Miharu joined the family, and Edith arrived a few years later. Grapevines were in their prime and production was at its peak, with price of table grapes soaring to record highs. My parents' perseverance and determination had begun to pay dividends.

To keep the chickens and jackrabbits from invading mother's vegetable garden, father had built a chicken wire fence around the garden. At two feet tall, it was high enough to keep out unwelcome visitors but low enough for an adult to step over the fence and into the garden, thereby eliminating the need for a gate. Mother had literally hopped over the fence hundreds of times to retrieve the vegetables with ease and grace, but as her latest pregnancy entered its final stage, her coordination suffered.

"Ouch!" said my mother as, eight months pregnant with me, she tripped over the fence. I executed a somersault in her womb. After torturous hours of pain, the midwife Mayeda delivered me feet first at eleven that evening, under the dim light of a 60-watt bulb hanging from the rafter.

The premature birth of his fifth child caught Father by surprise, and now he had the task of naming me. It was October 12, 1928. The Japanese identify years by combining the name for the era with the number of years the current emperor has ruled; it was Emperor Hirohito's third year of reign (*san* means three in Japanese), and during the era referred to as *Showa*.

"Showasan," Father contemplated as a possible name for me, since I was his third son born in the third year of *Showa*. But "That doesn't sound right," he told Mother. "How about Shosan? That's funny, too, but you could also pronounce the Japanese Kanji characters Shozo. We'll name him Shozo." My other name—Hank—would come later, through just as many twists.

The year 1928 was a prosperous time for California grape farmers, as well as for the nation in general. Father hired a carpenter to build a living room addition to the house, and he planted a willow tree in front. The economy of the entire country was at its peak, the stock market a mighty bull with not a hint of a bear in sight. The willow tree grew strong in reflection of the market.

Given that stock prices were rising without sufficient foundation in an era of seemingly unending prosperity, eventually the market had to tumble, and so it did on October 29, 1929. Depression was now the mood of the nation. Demand for Tokay table grapes began to plummet, and so did the prices. It was a sudden devastating event followed by an abrupt and unforeseen family tragedy.

Father was a chain smoker of Bull Durhams, which came in a small white cotton bag with supply of paper attached to the side. When he contracted a common cold, it turned into pneumonia because of a tainted lung, and one night, his heart stopped during his sleep. Father passed away in 1931, in the midst of the Great Depression, leaving mother with five children, the oldest son a mere fifteen years old, and the youngest—me—only two and a half. Mother had never dreamed this would be her life, and she was unprepared to confront it.

* * *

Hastily jumping back across the stream from that bogus Garden of Eden, I backtracked, looking for a sign in the fork. *Surely there must be a sign to keep the hikers on course*, I thought as I scanned the vicinity without success. Since it was a lightly traveled trail (I hadn't seen a fellow hiker all morning), I concluded that there might not be a trail sign at all. Just then I spotted an official

National Forest Service redwood sign nailed to a pine tree about ten feet above the ground.

"What kind of a fool would put a sign up there? We're no giants, you know," I grunted in disgust. It took several hours before it dawned on me that the sign had once been at eye level many years ago, before the tree had grown to its present height. The remainder of the trek was along chaparral terrain with colorful shrubbery dotting the landscape.

At the apex, along with a pile of large, jagged granite stones and an engraved wooden sign denoting that this was San Bernardino Peak, there was an olive drab ammo box, vintage military, attached by a cable to the monument. It was a sign-in box with a tablet filled with signatures of recent hikers. One recent entry read *Enjoyed the 8-mile hike to 10,624 feet peak. Sixty-two years old and I'll be back soon.* It was reassuring to know that there were other old-timers who were also tackling the local peaks, refusing to grow old.

I looked over to East San Bernardino Peak only half a mile away, wondering whether to hike there, but the weaker side of me was the victor that time. *I'm too tired today; I'll do it next time,* I thought to myself.

Descending the mountain, I encountered my first living soul of the day.

"How you doing?" he asked. He was brawny, an outdoorsy, nature-loving type in his early thirties. By the ease with which he strode up the trail, it was obvious he was a seasoned hiker.

"Not so good," I replied. "I was too tired to make it up to East San Bernardino Peak."

"Well, you could hike up from Momyer Creek or Forest Falls," he said and laughed. "The Forest Falls trail is fabulous, but hardly anyone uses it." He explained that the trail was approximately fourteen miles round-trip. He added, "But who's foolish enough to do that when you could just walk another fifteen minutes from San Bernardino Peak to reach East San Bernardino Peak?"

"Well, I'm stupid enough to attempt that Forest…whatever…trail," I sheepishly responded with a restrained laugh.

It turned out he was an off-duty forest ranger taking a casual walk up the mountain. After giving me detailed instructions for finding the Forest Falls trailhead, which he cautioned was extremely easy to miss, he momentarily stared at my white hair. Saluting me with a raised, clenched fist, he said, "You're young as long as you're young at heart!"

The following weekend, I was at the Forest Falls trailhead at six o'clock in the morning. The ranger was right: the East San Bernardino part was indeed difficult to find, and I had to backtrack a few hundred yards to spot the faint path veering off the main trail. I also noticed the grass growing on the surface of the narrow trail, with no sign of being trampled. *What if I'm injured or have a heart attack? I'm no spring chicken, and there won't be any hikers in the vicinity to find me.* This thought kept running through my mind as I stood contemplating whether to proceed further. It was a frightening thought that reminded me of Mother being widowed with five young children in an unfamiliar land with an unpredictable future cast only in fragile hopes and dreams. Surely she must have had many "what if" questions on her mind. Perhaps that was one of the reasons she returned to her birthplace several months after Father's death to visit her mother for emotional comfort and support.

* * *

A year later, after erecting a headstone for Father in Japan, Mother left my sisters Miharu and Edith with my aunts there and returned to Florin with Ben, Sam, and me. I never asked Mother why she left my sisters in Japan, but I'm sure she had a valid reason for doing so. Upon returning, Ben, at sixteen, left school and took over the farm chores. Mother helped, doing everything from feeding the family from the vegetable garden to harvesting the grapes. She took a shovel in her hand and irrigated the vineyard; she hammered the nails with uninterrupted rhythm, making thousands of crates for shipping; she harvested grapes from sunrise to sundown, then packed them in crates, a task that usually lasted until midnight. The only things she didn't do were harness the horses and plow the vineyard.

Kneeling and wiping her forehead, Mother burned dried grapevines in a sod stove, a *hetsuisan*, constructed of mud and hay. This was no ordinary mud but adobe soil from the northern sector of our ranch. This soil became hard as brick and impenetrable when dry, and slick, sticky, and compacted when wet, turning a day into a nightmare during every plowing season. I often accompanied Ben to the blacksmith shop to get our broken plow repaired whenever it fell victim to the adobe, or "hard pan" as the local farmers often referred to the clay loam. Yet hard pan, which both Ben and Father had cursed and damned for twenty years, was one of the building blocks of our life. When repairing our three-burner *hetsuisan* kiln, I had the lowly job of stomping my bare feet in the mixture of adobe, hay, and water in a large washtub until the pieces of hay were thoroughly mixed in, to give the kiln body and strength.

During those years after Father's death, we still managed to eat well. For everyday meals, we'd often have *chiri-chiri,* as mother called her chicken sukiyaki dinner. Sukiyaki was derived from the word *suki,* meaning plow, and *yaki,* meaning cook. During Japan's early history, when people lived primarily on fish and vegetables, eating meat was considered a taboo, hence people refrained from cooking it indoors and did it outdoors over a fire using a plow as a skillet. I often wonder if that troubled cultural relationship to meat was the reason why our family didn't have much meat in our daily diet during my childhood years. Was it that, or was it simply because we couldn't afford to buy meat?

After our evening meals, we took turns having a bath. Like many other Japanese families in the countryside, we had a stand-alone bathhouse, or *furoba*. Standing on the cement floor of the structure, we washed our bodies with soap and hot water before entering the actual tub, which was made of thick, rust-colored redwood. It was deep and rectangular, resting on a U-shaped adobe foundation in which dried grapevines were burned to heat the water. A latticed redwood platform, or *gesu-ita*, protected our bodies from being singed by the galvanized metal sheet covering the bottom of the tub. Gray water was recycled by draining it into the flowerbeds and vegetable garden.

When we left the door of the bathhouse open, we could see the graceful olive tree and the fragrant red and white flowering oleander shrubs. As we came out, there was a young date palm to the right and a cluster of red cannas bordered by purple and pink flowering ice plants. In the springtime the surrounding landscape was splattered golden with California poppies.

It was in this bathhouse that I had my first lessons before attending Sierra School. Mother wrote my name, "Shozo," on the side of the redwood bathtub with her wet index finger. Several nights later, she wrote "Umemoto." I copied those words on the tub over and over for the next several evenings to prepare for that first day of school.

When Ben took me to school for the first time, class was already in session.

Miss Bolton wrote "Shozo" in her notebook and nodded goodbye to Ben as he departed. She assigned me the third desk on the right row, which definitely must have been a low spot on the floor, since I soon noticed liquid trickling toward my feet from the desk in front of me. As Sierra School served a predominantly Japanese population, in which Japanese was the primary language spoken at home, only a few of the first-graders were able to communicate such an intricate phrase as "May I go to the lavatory?" The boy sitting in front of me fell into that category.

It took months for us to learn just the basic phrases for communication. Perhaps this is why after finishing first grade we had to spend another year in High First before proceeding to second grade. It wasn't until I was in my teens that I learned I had actually flunked first grade and High First was merely the euphemistic term for the remedial class.

Milk Tops was one of the favorite games among boys during those early years. It was played with the cardboard caps from milk bottles. Each player puts a bottle cap into the pot, like the ante in a poker game. Then each player tosses a cap against the wall of a building, like a penny pitch, and whoever comes closest to the wall has the first chance to throw all the caps high over his head. Whichever caps landed face up belonged to him. The boy whose cap was second-closest to the wall then did the same thing with the remaining tops. The process continued until there were no milk tops left.

I remember a particular day when one boy was unlucky and irked. "Goddamn," he shouted, followed by, "*Bakatare!*" (Stupid!) These bilingual curses at the top of his lungs didn't please the teachers, and all five of us were called into a small first aid room, where each boy was instructed to rub his index finger on a bar of white soap and wash out his mouth. I was the last in line.

"You don't have to wash your mouth. You may go, Shozo," the teacher said.

"Hey, I didn't have to wash out my mouth," I told my classmates.

"You're a big liar!" they accused me.

Being *labeled* a liar certainly did not agree with me, so I decided that I'd lie and tell everybody that I *had* washed out my mouth, so no one would think I was fibbing.

In 1992, Sierra School held a fifty-year reunion. (It had been fifty years since the World War II evacuation in 1942.) While looking at the old class picture, I pointed myself out to the teacher who had been involved in the soap incident.

"Oh, you were so cute," she remarked. Could it possibly have been that I didn't have to wash my mouth with soap because I was cute?

There were three female teachers at Sierra School. All in their early twenties, they were dedicated to their jobs, taking whatever means necessary to teach us the language that would help us assimilate and succeed in this nation's economy and society. As a result of their devotion, we heeded their wishes and began to speak the language. At Japanese language school, however, Yoshikawa Sensei was just as dedicated to teaching his subject matter. Noticing that we were speaking English on the playground, he committed a good portion of the class to admonishing us that we were to speak Japanese whenever we were on Japanese School premises. Thus life was beginning to push us in complicated and contradictory directions, leading to feelings of cultural schizophrenia.

Meanwhile, at home, the redwood bathtub wall continued to be my blackboard. Two plus two equals four, multiplication tables, and pictures of funny faces and stick people covered the sides of the tub. As the smoldering embers turned to ash and the hot water turned lukewarm, I would leave all my worries, troubles, complications, and mixed emotions in the bathhouse. Later, under my *futon*, I felt fully relaxed and comfortable, ready for a pleasant dream and another bright tomorrow.

Another place of rest was a *suzumen*, a wooden platform the size of a double bed and about fifteen inches high that my Father had built. He was apparently inspired by his parents' house in Japan, where the floor was elevated about fifteen inches from the ground. There was a walkway along the rear of the house, an extension of the floor, like a patio, where they often lounged, drinking tea and gazing into the rear garden during the warm summer evenings. Father's version, called a *suzumen*, probably derived from the word *suzumu*, meaning to cool off, and *men*, meaning a surface.

As autumn approached, cucumbers faded yellow, carrots and onions turned to stalks, and dozens of other vegetables went to seed. Mother painstakingly selected the best of the crop and dried their seeds on this *suzumen* bench to prepare for the next season's crop. This is where she sat to peel persimmons and hang them tiered on a string, like a fisherman stringing his catch on a chain, allowing them to dry until the fruit turned snowy white from the sugar within.

The *suzumen* was good for working but also for relaxing. The warm spring weather was ideal for just lying on this wide bench for a midday nap, and many summer evenings were spent on it lounging around reminiscing, as well as dreaming of the promising future.

* * *

Continuing on the trail to East San Bernardino Peak, the thought crossed my mind that the complete absence of other hikers in the area probably wouldn't have stopped my parents from hiking this route. With renewed confidence, I decided to continue on up the rarely treaded trail. The terrain was moderate in the beginning, but as I approached the midpoint, I could see the steep ascent as it neared the crest. Then I saw two hikers coming down the trail. I was so relieved to find I wasn't the only one on the trail that I felt an urge to jump up in joy. I waved and waited until we met on the trail.

"Am I glad to see you guys!" I was gleaming with elation. "For a while, I thought I was the last person on earth."

"You don't know how glad we are to see you!" a fiftyish

woman exclaimed while her male companion nodded in agreement. "We're looking for East San Bernardino Peak," she added. Her name was Kate.

"You're going the wrong way," I said and pointed behind them. We all laughed and resumed the hike toward the peak together, exchanging notes and experiences. The local mountains are a maze of trails, and apparently they had started on the other side of the mountain and were proceeding down on this side of the mountain. During the course of the conversation, I mentioned my fantasy of climbing Mount Whitney someday.

"I'd like to make it up Whitney one day, too, but unfortunately, I have a bad heart and am taking medication," Kate said.

"What kind of a heart condition?" I asked.

"My heart beats at about thirty-eight per minute."

"What's wrong with that? Some of the greatest athletes have a heartbeat at thirty-eight. Doesn't it mean you have a strong heart?"

Kate smiled and shook her head.

At the summit and enjoying a snack while we continued to chat about Mount Whitney, a hiker in his mid-twenties approached from San Bernardino Peak and joined us in the conversation.

"Back in the 1970s, I remember hearing about a sixty-year-old lady running up Mount Whitney in her sneakers, and I understand that she kept hiking Whitney into her eighties," I said.

"Yeah, my grandmother was a good friend of hers. She hiked Whitney over twenty times and passed away recently, at age one hundred and four in Yucaipa," the hiker said.

"Wow!" I said. "And I have a tough time climbing this one. I'll never make it up Whitney!" I said with conviction. I was excited and satisfied just to meet a hiker whose grandmother was a friend of a woman who had hiked Whitney more than twenty times. I was astounded at the wonders of a human body that can sustain so much and attain so many things that might appear to be absolute impossibilities.

During the ensuing years, I often met Kate hiking solo on the trails, always taking a few minutes to have a pleasant chat. One day she said, "I made it up Whitney last week." I was just as thrilled and ecstatic as she was that she had made it despite her heart condition.

Descending the mountain, I couldn't help but be reminded of Mother, who came to America as a frail young bride with a diseased lung. Despite her initial weakness, she was always on the move, without a moment of idleness. I have always admired how she and Father built a home and a life on a piece of barren land with nothing but their bare hands, pure guts, and determination.

Chapter Three

A DAY IN THE LIFE OF A HOBO

At six in the morning, there were already fifteen hikers lined up in front of Mentone Ranger Station to obtain a permit to enter the San Gorgonio Wilderness Area and climb Old Grayback (San Gorgonio Mountain) via Vivian Creek Trail. Forty permits were issued every day for that popular route, and when that quota was filled, hikers could take the less strenuous but longer twenty-one-mile (round-trip) South Fork Trail to San Gorgonio Peak. The less popular San Bernardino Peak Trail, among the very best I have walked, almost always had permits available. For the even less popular Momyer and Forsee Creek Trails, the permit applications were simply placed on the outdoor table as self-issues. As I filled out the permit for Momyer Creek Trail, my favorite, I wondered why so many people line up for permits to hike Vivian Creek Trail, which was essentially a wilderness highway, congested with overnight campers and day hikers, and by no means an escape to solitude.

I stopped the truck in an open parking area by the San Bernardino mountainside and gazed into the sky. There was not a fleck of cloud, and I forecast this balmy July morning would turn into a hot and dry day. I was at 5,400 feet and my destination, East San Bernardino Peak, was just another 4,900 feet higher, and probably a bit cooler, but not cold enough to warrant lugging my usual hiking gear. I emptied my backpack of a Gortex jacket, gloves, and instep crampons to lighten my load, keeping only a light parka to protect myself from the elements.

Without the runoff in the summer, Momyer Creek did not have much water, and crossing the creek was a breeze. As I hopped on the rocks, I noticed gold mica glistening in the stream.

"Fool's gold!" I laughed out loud and remembered one summer when I was a child in Florin, wrapped in an aura of fantasy and imagination.

* * *

"Little Red Riding Hood" may have been a favorite story among the girls I knew, but Captain Kidd and his buried treasure was far more intriguing for us boys. As summer vacation approached, I was ready for three months of adventure, Captain Kidd-style, with rubies and silver and, of course, gold!

The summer I was eight years old, mother and I were by ourselves on the farm during the sweltering heat of the day and beneath the flicker of stars and the soothing glare of moonlight at night. Both my sisters were still in Japan, and Ben and Sam were picking pears in a nearby orchard area called Loomis to supplement our family income.

Mother began the day at sunrise, making crates for the upcoming grape harvesting season, with *thump thump, thump-thump-thump* beats like a musical rhythm that continued well into the afternoon. I assisted her by soaking the ends of the slats in water to prevent the wood from cracking as she hammered the nails with a symphonic grace and ease that made me believe she was doing it as entertainment rather than as a necessary chore.

By late afternoon, the temperature had subsided enough so that the water would seep into the ground instead of evaporating into the scorching atmosphere, and that meant it was time to irrigate the vineyard. As Mother turned on the water pump, the whining and the whirling noise of a dome-shaped seven-horsepower electric motor filled the pump shed and, after a minute, sent a gush of water spurting out the pipe with a thunderous whoosh and a splash. Water flowed down the dry canal like an arrow. I followed the stream until it eventually found its way into the rows and rows of irrigation ditches carved between the grapevines. It was past suppertime before the first several rows were saturated with water. Mother diverted the flow into the next set of ditches and continued the process well past midnight.

In the days that followed, I had my turn at making crates. I took a set of slats and a handful of four-penny nails and began to hammer. Crooked and bent, my first several boxes stood out like sore thumbs among the neatly stacked crates my mother had made, and it wasn't long before—"Ouch!" The hammer struck my thumb instead of the nail. Not wanting mother to notice the accident, I stepped out of the barn quietly and nonchalantly, and found a secluded area in the vineyard to cry. Squeezing my thumb with my right hand, I rolled over in the dirt again and again, and finally ran like a deranged child with no destination in mind. I did everything to ease the pain, but nothing was working. When I found myself by the irrigation pump shed, I lay flat on my stomach and dipped my thumb into the water gushing along the main ditch. The cold water from the well seemed to have a soothing, numbing effect in the 102-degree temperature. Finding refuge under a statuesque chestnut tree, its straight, outstretched branches casting a gigantic shade, I felt a gentle breeze, and the pain became almost bearable. As I gazed into the eddy that formed as the water rushed out the well, it was enough to lead me into a comfortable, relaxing hypnotic trance.

Suddenly, I stood up, heart pounding, forgetting about the sore thumb as I stared at the glittering flakes swirling in the pool. It was gold! I walked along each irrigation ditch until signs of the golden flakes disappeared, carefully mapping out in my mind the area of gold-bearing soil. I ran to the house for an empty strawberry jelly jar, and on my hands and knees in the dirt I began the painstaking task of picking up one flake at a time.

"I'm going to keep it a secret," I whispered, "until I have a jar-ful." I then decided that I'd buy a Caterpillar 22 tractor for plowing to replace the two horses for Ben. For my mother, I'd get a kerosene stove so she wouldn't have to light the dry grapevine brush under the adobe kiln at every mealtime. And for myself, I'd purchase a couple of wing-tipped Oxford shoes.

I loosened a plank in the pump shed floor and hid the jar for the evening. Excited, I hardly slept that night.

After getting up in the morning and placing a wad of newspaper in my shoe, which was showing a tiny hole in the sole, I embarked on my usual daily ritual, being careful not to appear conspicuous during the hour or two I spent amassing my treasure. As summer vacation was nearing its end, the jar was about a quarter full with the glittering flakes. The hole in my sole was getting larger, my smashed thumbnail had fallen off and a new nail was beginning to take its place. Mother had made more than three thousand crates. She was now in front of her Singer sewing machine making my shirts and jeans for the new school year, and it was also time for my brothers to return home to begin the grape harvesting. The days were getting shorter, and the task of collecting the golden glitters had to be postponed until next summer.

Before long, it was already January—time to relax, eat, drink and be merry, visit the neighbors, and entertain our friends for the traditional celebration of the first seven days of the New Year.

"Shozo," Sam called me. "Put your good clothes on. We're going *ohaka-mairi* (visiting gravesites) with some of my friends." This was not a traditional activity, but it would make a nice outing and a nice way to spend the day with his friends. Our pilgrimage to gravesites took us to the resting place of a young girl named Okei, alleged to be one of the first Japanese to immigrate to the United States, and the first one to pass away in this new country. Then we went to nearby Coloma, the site where James W. Marshall first discovered gold, leading to the great gold rush of 1848 and 1849. The history exhibit there included pictures, mining tools, and two vials of gold resting side by side in a glass showcase framed in dark wood. One vial contained dull gold pebbles, but the other had shiny, sparkling gold-colored flakes exactly like the ones I had gathered from our irrigation ditches! I felt my face turning red with excitement.

I was speechless as the attendant approached me. I was expecting him to tell me that the sparkling golden flakes were real gold, but he pointed at them and commented, "Fool's gold."

"Fool's gold?" I suddenly got the impression that something was awfully wrong.

"Yes. This is real gold." He pointed to the vial containing the tiny bits of pale golden granules, totally different in shape and appearance than what I had accumulated in my jar.

"How much is this fool's gold worth?"

"Nothing."

"Not even one hundred dollars?"

"Not even a penny!" He laughed.

I returned home a bit wiser but in despair. I lifted the loose plank from the pump shed floor and stared solemnly at the jar. As I strolled to the ditch under the chestnut where I had first discovered the flakes, the setting sun cast a diffused streak of hazy rays through the bare tree branches, and the ditch where there once was a crystal clear pool of swirling water was now covered with dry stalks of light brown barn grass. The golden mica fluttered and glistened as I emptied the jar. The flakes floated gently on the breeze, showering the lifeless grass and leaving a glittery residue on the wing-tipped Oxfords Ben had bought me, reminding me how fortunate I was that I didn't have to walk around barefoot like some of the neighbor kids.

I got everything I need. I didn't want that gold anyway! All these years later, however, I wonder if I was just rationalizing, or if it was really possible that some people honored and lived by the philosophy that they truly had everything they needed? I once met a hobo who seemed to be content with everything he had, which wasn't much. Was that his philosophy? His worldly possessions were stuffed in a gunnysack he carried over his shoulder. This was during the era the nation was recovering from the Great Depression.

FDR promised to put people to work through government programs, and the New Deal jobs, through the Works Progress Administration (WPA), were in evidence everywhere. The WPA, established under the Emergency Relief Act of April 1935, built 650,000 miles of hard-surfaced roads and constructed 80,000 new bridges. WPA workers tore down the wooden bridge on Bradshaw Road, in front of our farm, and replaced it with a concrete structure. They also dug drainage ditches and asphalted several miles of dirt road that passed in front of our vineyard.

Evidence of hard times was everywhere. It was a late Saturday morning when the hobo wandered onto our farm, asking for something to eat. I'd seen hobos trudging the two-lane highways a number times, but this was the first time I'd personally met one close-up. I wondered how exciting it would be to roam the countryside without destination, carefree and not a speck of worry on my mind. *What an adventure!* I thought as I watched him sitting on a crate and munching the strawberry sandwiches Mother had made for him.

I later had the same for lunch, except my sandwich was made from the heels of the loaf of bread. "How come I get the ears and that tramp got the good pieces?" I asked.

"Remember," she replied as she ate her *ochazuke* (tea poured over rice), "you must always give the nicer and larger pieces to others, and you should eat the leftovers."

"Even a tramp?"

She didn't answer.

Well, I guess he's human, too, I thought.

This was early spring and the vineyards and surrounding pastures were covered with green grass seedlings making their debut. Row after row of grapevines were budding. Everything seemed to suddenly bloom into life after the cold winter freeze, transforming the landscape into its most beautiful and picturesque. Snow white mushroom heads appeared from under cow dung in our neighbor Mr. Barnby's green pasture. Buckets in our hands, Mother and I picked the mushrooms—but only the flat, pure white ones, since the round dome-shaped ones with dark undersides were poisonous. *Pop, pop,* the mushroom stems snapped as we pulled them up.

Once while we were picking mushrooms within the vicinity of the newly WPA-constructed Bradshaw Bridge, I went down the bank and under the bridge and found a pile of hay.

"So this is where the hobo slept that night," I said. I examined the pile, leveled it, and lay down on the makeshift pad.

"Wow! What a life," I said to myself. "Don't have to study, don't have to brush my teeth, there's nobody to tell me to get up in the morning, and I could spread my wings and travel all around the country, and even the whole world."

The warm afternoon temperature was mesmerizing, and I let my imagination be whisked away to cloud nine. But it wasn't long before the sun shifted behind the oak trees, and as I started to feel chilly, I felt a tickling sensation on the back of my hand. Suddenly both arms were covered with goose pimples and my scalp was tingling as if the hairs were standing on their ends. Aside from snakes, there are no creatures I fear more than centipedes, and here were two of them crawling on my arm. I darted away from the bridge, trembling as I desperately tried to shake off the critters.

Later that evening, while I burned the brush under the *furoba* to heat the bathwater, my heart started pumping again as I recalled the centipedes creeping over my body. I finally calmed down after a long, hot bath. Back in my colorful bedroom, wallpapered with newspapers, I snuck under my *futon* and watched the torn pages intermittently sway to and fro in the gentle evening breeze that seeped through the cracks in the wall. I realized how fortunate I was that I had a comfortable home and not a worry in the world of ever being hungry.

* * *

This day, crossing the fool's gold filled Momyer Creek, I continued on the trail and veered left onto a seldom traveled path leading to East San Bernardino Peak. It was toward the end of summer, and with a clear sky and a predawn temperature reading in the comfortable 60s, it was an ideal hiking day. By eight o'clock, it began to feel warm. *Going to be a hot day today.* By nine, scattered puffy clouds began to appear overhead. I recalled the previous evening's TV forecast having mentioned a monsoon approaching Southern California from the Baja coast. As the cloud formation increased with each step I took up the trail, I concluded that it was going to be not only hot but miserably muggy. I gazed at the huge white cloud front looming in the south but kept assuring myself that there was no such thing as a monsoon in Southern California, no matter what the weatherman had said.

Ignoring the advancing clouds, I continued on. I had traveled this trail several times before, but on this day the landscape, including the narrow trail, was covered with beautiful ground-hugging pink and purple flowers. I was stomping and squashing the tiny blooms as I trekked toward the summit, and although I don't mind crushing grass and weeds, stepping on dazzlingly colorful flowers felt different. Eventually my conscience began to bother me and I became infused with guilt, probably because Chiyoko treats flowers and plants as living, breathing beings and was constantly reminding me to do the same.

Issei folks often talked about *bachi*, a bad omen in consequence of wrongdoing. *Bachi* is a punishment that comes back to us in many forms, sometimes without warning, at any time in the near or distant future. *Would this curse apply to hurting beautiful flowers and plants? They're living, too*, I mused, as I began to tread more lightly and carefully as I continued on the trail.

Since I was well on my way to a ten-thousand-foot peak, it may have been altitude sickness that caused my mind to enter the realm of superstition. Altitude sickness comes in various forms; there have been many times I've felt like I was high on drugs. I remember once when I heard a hiker approaching me from the rear saying, "You better take a rest. You almost fell." I glanced to the left and there was a steep cliff into the valley below. It suddenly occurred to me that I was indeed woozy and needed a break. Another time I hiked down a mountain with a friend who kept asking me every time we sat on a large rock to rest, "Hank, are we in a motel now?" He was hallucinating.

"Yeah, hang in there, we're almost there," I kept encouraging him, although it was two o'clock in the morning and we were in a dark forest at 10,000 feet and twenty miles from his motel.

* * *

It was definitely not a mere hallucination the day I experienced *bachi* firsthand after I stole seven cents when I was still in elementary school. On weekends, my friend Howard regularly walked half a mile down Bradshaw Road to buy chocolate candy bars at Walsh Station, a lone convenience store with a hand-operated gas pump situated at a crossroads amid the grape vineyards. Before I left, I took seven pennies from our family's *osaisenbako*, a box where Buddhists deposit coins when worshipping. The money is an offering to thank Buddha for prayers that were answered. The box was placed in front of our *Butsudan*, our small household shrine.

Coins in hand, I went to Walsh Station and bought a handful of lemon drops. I wasn't home long before mother detected a bulge in my pocket and gave me a long lecture about how it was considered bad manners to want something that someone else has; besides, candy was bad for my teeth and health. Most importantly, though, it was absolutely sinful and despicable to steal from Buddha, she said.

"It's only seven cents," I argued.

"Seven cents or seven dollars, it doesn't make any difference," she said. "*Bachi ga atarimasu.*" (Bad things will happen to you.) She was committed to deterring me from a life of crime, or a miserable "next life," since many Buddhists followed the philosophy that if you do wrong as a human, you will be reborn as a lowly animal or a slimy reptile.

Surprisingly, Mother felt that satisfying my desires would be the best measure to prevent me from stealing. When I accompanied her to Yorozu Dry Goods in Sacramento the following weekend, she bought a box of five hundred Butter Balls, incorrectly assuming that they were made from butter and weren't bad for the teeth. Although I could have sworn it looked like candy and tasted like candy, I was willing to accept her words unequivocally.

While Mother was looking through some yardage to make our new shirts, trousers, and underwear, the saleslady stroked my head and commented, "What nice, soft brown hair." She meant it as a compliment, but to Mother, it was an insult. *Only hakujin (white people) have brown hair; Japanese have black hair,* she thought. She nevertheless eked out a polite smile, but I found out later that it was not a sincere gesture because as soon as we returned home she took out the electric hair clippers and clipped me nearly *bozu* (bald) against my will. She reasoned that darker hair would emerge after each clipping and I would eventually have black hair like other Japanese boys.

Monday morning, she slipped two Butter Balls in my pocket and walked with me to the end of our farm's barbed wire fence to see me off to school. As usual, I was taking a shortcut through grape vineyards, hay fields, and pastures. But on this day, in the recently harvested hay field, I came across six longhorn bulls that were to be used in the upcoming Barnby's Rodeo show. As soon as I crossed the fence into the field, they stood up, formed a straight line, and faced me as though they were going to rush me any second. It was frightening; my knees were knocking and weak. I took a deep breath and ran as fast as I could across the field, through the muddy puddle in the creek bed, and into my friend Tad's vineyard. Once behind the barbed wire fence, I ran straight to his house, trembling and never looking back. *Is this the* bachi *Mother warned me about?* I wondered.

Looking at my *bozu* head, some of my schoolmates grinned and giggled softly, and some others stared, but everyone was polite, at least until after lunch, when I stuck two Butter Balls in my mouth. With my round face, *bozu* haircut, and a Butter Ball in each cheek, I must have looked hilarious, and it didn't take much imagination for them to nickname me "One Hundred Butter Ball." But I only had two in my mouth, so why did they call me "One Hundred Butter Balls," I wondered.

En route to Japanese School, I related my experience with the bulls to my friends. I bent my knees and leaned forward with both hands beside my forehead, fingers pointing out like horns. I kicked my right foot, ready to attack. Soon, five of us boys were all doing it in a straight line across the road, and when the Minami sisters, driving home from Sacramento High School, tried to pass by, we ferociously postured like bulls, huffed and stomped our feet and blocked the road to prevent them from passing. The Minami sister in the driver's seat stopped and asked us to make way for their car. Exasperated, she blew her horn and shouted. We knew then that it was time for us to retreat. It was fun; it gave us an unbelievable sense of power, even if only momentarily, and we repeated the attack on their vehicle for the rest of the week. It wasn't until later that I realized it must have upset them deeply.

Returning home from school that Friday, I sensed something strange about Mother and Ben—they certainly weren't in their usual mood. They waited until after supper to bring up what was bothering them.

"Sho-*chan*," Mother began, "Minami-*san* was here today and…" A long lecture followed, covering every aspect of our crime. Was being reprimanded a *bachi*, too? I wondered. If it were, I'd received two *bachi* so far and that should be the last of it. I felt guilty, ashamed, and sorry. Sad and depressed, I spent the Saturday morning around the irrigation pump shed and finally lay facedown on a clover patch, looking for a four-leaf clover.

"Nope, not a lucky day," I mumbled to myself.

Then suddenly I remembered the honey beehive deeply hidden inside a pile of dead grape trunks that I'd been instructed never to approach. Miserable and lonely, and somehow angered,

I took a stick and started poking the beehive. A few bees appeared and buzzed overhead. Then some more. And then I felt a sting on my head. Whenever a bee stings, it leaves a pheromone, a scent that lures other bees to attack. That bee must have left a big batch of pheromones because now the rest were swarming all over me. A bite on the arm followed, and another sting on my vulnerable *bozu* head. I felt a sting every two seconds, and as I ran toward the house, I could see the buzzing cloud of bees following overhead. When I reached the house, I was finally free.

First, I felt only a dull pain from all the bee stings. Several days later, the pain intensified, turning to unbearable itching pain, and my scratching then turned the bites into an ugly mess of pus on my head. Weeks of scratching, pain, and agony—all starting from the theft of the seven pennies and ending with this *bachi*. At least one happy thing came out of this ordeal besides learning some hard lessons: I never had to get a *bozu* haircut again.

* * *

Continuing to tread tenderly on the floral carpeted trail to East San Bernardino peak, I noticed that the monsoon cloud front was directly overhead. I proceeded up the steepest climb of the trail and arrived at a plateau with tall pine trees. I welcomed the light raindrops that began to sprinkle my T-shirt; it was invigorating. When it began to pour, I took out my lightweight parka and wished that I had brought my heavier Gortex jacket. Soon I saw a flash of light, followed almost instantly with a crackle and thunder. At ten thousand feet, the lightning was almost directly overhead, too close for comfort; it was the first time in my life I had experienced an almost simultaneous flash and boom. I instinctively selected the tallest tree on the plateau and took cover.

While standing under the tree thinking that it was a safe haven, I recalled what my hiking friend Craig had once shown me. Craig is a big fellow; both of my feet can probably fit into one of his shoes. With long white hair and a beard, he looked like a hippie who hadn't visited a barber for thirty years. A retired physicist and an intellect, he always stopped a few times on his hiking trail not to rest but to read books while enjoying the fresh pine-scented air and the splendor of mountain scenery. We often hiked together, and one day he pointed to a pine tree off the trail and said, "I was standing right here when it happened." I looked at the tree, which had a jagged bare spot on the trunk about twelve feet above the ground. I guesstimated that it was less than a hundred feet away from where we stood. The white bare spot was about eighteen inches long and about ten inches wide. I stared at the spot wondering what had happened.

"That's kind of high for a bear claw mark," I said.

"Lightning struck and the barks were flying," he said and laughed, probably at my stupid remark.

After recalling Craig's incident, and grasping the concept that taking cover under a tall tree in an open area during a lightning storm is an invitation to trouble, I scurried away from the shelter.

The thunderstorm over San Bernardino Mountain was soon over, with hot summer sun turning raindrops on the low-lying manzanita bushes into an aura of shimmering steam rising into the atmosphere. I stood on the plateau and gazed into the valley below. The wilted flowers on the trail were being rejuvenated by the downpour and starting to perk up. I concluded that I would not receive a *bachi* for trampling on them after all. Yet, the ridiculous image of me with a *bozu* head, Butter Balls in my cheeks, and the deserved moniker of "One Hundred Butter Ball" lingered on. It wasn't the only time my embarrassment was tied to a large number. Another vivid boyhood memory bubbled to the surface.

* * *

Whenever our neighbor Art came to visit Ben, he always brought me the comic books he had finished reading. Art was a pre-med student at Berkeley, but had been forced to drop out of school when his father became ill. As a child, I thought he read comic books because he was smart; I hadn't seen any other farmers—mostly without college educations—being addicted to comic books, so it seemed a logical conclusion at the time. Whenever Ben took me to Sacramento, I always bought a ten-cent comic book hoping I would become smart like Art.

One day, Art handed me the May issue of *Detective Comics*. One fascinating story featured a boy a few years younger than I whose parents were murdered by a hoodlum. As an adult, this boy became a crime-fighting masked crusader. People called him the Batman. Completely enthralled, I read the story a dozen times before it ended up as my personal toilet tissue. (Our recycling habits made us the "green" people of our generation.)

Decades later, in 1982, while visiting the then-famous nation's largest swap meet in Quartzsite, Arizona, I came across a comic book dealer with a very large collection. While browsing through his stock, I casually mentioned that I once owned a 1939 issue of *Detective Comics* #27.

"I used it as toilet paper," I confessed as I lowered my head in embarrassment.

He looked stunned and then started laughing.

"One…" he started, then began laughing so hard he couldn't finish his sentence.

"One hundred thou—" he kept trying.

Finally, he was able to complete what he wanted to say: "One-hundred-thousand-dollar asshole!" It was the mid-eighties, and that was the issue in which Batman was introduced. It was selling for a whopping one hundred thousand dollars. I swallowed my pride and joined in on the laughter.

After completing the tour of the swap meet, Chiyoko and I found an isolated area in the nearby desert to park our motorhome for the night. I took an evening hike with Chiko under a crimson sky rippled with cirrus clouds. The spectacular Arizona sunset appeared like the bloody red fires of hell. I said to Chiko, "You know, I don't mind being an ordinary, run-of-the-mill asshole, but being a one-hundred-thousand-dollar asshole is sure hard to take." Chiko, a man's best friend, just ignored my sob story and kept on walking, intently looking for another rabbit to chase. Her complete apathy had hurt my feelings, but I guess it takes a hundred-thousand-dollar asshole to expect sympathy from a dog!

* * *

As I descended the mountain and returned to the trailhead, I noticed the thunderstorm runoff had changed the creek; the water level was much higher, and hopping across on boulders was no longer an option. Wading across the stream was the only alternative. I crossed with no trouble, and drenched with water up to my thighs, I hurried up to the parking area, which was about five minutes away. When I got there I was stunned.

I could have sworn that I'd parked the truck on asphalt, not dirt, but all I could see now was my blue truck sitting on top of silt, with no other vehicle in sight. Closer up, it became apparent that the flash flood down the canyon had swept a layer of mud, debris, stones, and small boulders onto the parking area.

"At least with my four-by-four, getting out of here will be no sweat," I said, but a more thorough assessment revealed that the entrance to the parking area was flooded two feet deep with mud and debris, and strewn with two-foot boulders. Even my four-wheel drive with oversized tires would not be able to maneuver through the barricade.

Fortunately, the lot was across a main mountain thoroughfare, and a bulldozer was soon clearing the area. Even more fortunate was that my truck was not on the other side of the road under the canyon; that could have caused some serious difficulties, like my truck receiving an unwelcome free ride along with the debris. Another small bulldozer appeared and helped clear the way. After three hours, I was finally on the road for my sixty-mile drive home. Taking consolation that at least my shoes and pants were partially dry by then, I was amazed at how frightening and devastating such an innocent-looking midsummer shower could be, and I wondered in retrospect if taking shelter alone in an open area atop a mountain peak during the thunderstorm was the proper thing to do.

I believe that if there is such a thing as a *bachi* for trudging on flowers, I certainly would have felt a zap accompanied by thunder.

* * *

Life is like a meandering stream, with joy and sorrow, and adventures and surprises lurking around every bend. There's the false glory of fool's gold; the hair-raising experience with the centipedes; the stings of bees and the recycled comic books worth a fortune. I have had my share of obstacles from time to time, but nature has usually been there for me, even if sometimes only in the form of memory. Maybe, in that way, I am a modern-day hobo, wandering through the mountains of California.

Chapter Four

THE NIGHT I SLEPT WITH DAISY

One of the criteria for successful hiking is to travel as light as possible, and that rule definitely influences what kind of flashlight I carry on my treks. *There are flashlights of all sizes, but what's the smallest I can have without getting lost in the dark?* I pondered this as I studied the descriptions of flashlights on display at REI.

I recalled the time I took my family on a tour of Moaning Cave in Vallecito many years ago. We were hoisted down by a crane in a cage, accompanied by a tour guide, and as we descended into the cave, it became cold and dank. When we reached the bottom, the entrance was closed and the cave became pitch black.

"Put your finger in front of your face and bring it toward your nose, but don't touch your nose," we heard a voice. My finger hit my nose and I still wasn't able to see my finger. "Now, that's total darkness," the tour guide said. She lit a match and the cave seemed to explode with light, as though a million floodlights were suddenly focused on us. She looked amused as she witnessed the surprised expressions on our faces.

With that experience emblazoned on my mind, and after long

deliberation in front of the flashlight display at the store, I finally decided to purchase a penlight powered by a single AA battery no larger than my little finger, compact and featherweight, since I was convinced that all I needed to light up a dark forest would be just a single candlepower.

Having been accustomed to the luxury of electric light bulbs all my life, and having lived in an urban area during most of my adult years, with streetlamps illuminating the surroundings from dusk to dawn, I had forgotten about the darkness of my childhood, when the only light at night was from the moon and the stars. When Mother realized one evening that her flashlight batteries were dead, she took a match out of her pocket to light her way. She always had a handful of wooden matchsticks for starting the fire in the kiln and lighting the brush under the Japanese bathtub. Holding the lit match in her hand, she groped her way in the faint light for a kerosene lamp hanging on the wall in the barn, bumping against crates and dusting equipment and feeling her way along the packing bench to guide her to the lamp.

Like fumbling across the barn in the semidarkness, feeling the way was probably the style of life for our parents as they tried to survive in a strange, unfamiliar country, where culture and language were an ocean apart from everything they knew. Their life was like seeking in the dark for the light that was their dreams becoming realities. They brushed against unforeseen obstacles not by choice but through necessity, all in an effort to eke out an existence from whatever resources were available.

* * *

Every year in early spring, the grape vineyard was covered with colorful wildflowers, including California poppy and plants with dark yellow flowers similar to the color of mustard, which led us to nickname them mustard grass.

"Help me pick the mustard grass buds," Mother said as she handed me a small bucket. My job was to hold the pail as she snipped the buds off the tall weeds. "I'm going to make *tsukemono*."

Her vegetable garden wasn't doing well that year. As a temporary measure to bridge the gap, she turned to what they had done when they first arrived from Japan and literally lived off the land. My initial thought was, *Make* tsukemono *from mustard grass? Tsukemono from weeds? Ugh!*

Reluctantly I helped gather the buds, visualizing the agony of having to eat the wild weeds with my *ochazuke*. Mustard grass buds were placed in our five-gallon vat with a liberal sprinkling of rock salt. A flat piece of wood was placed over the buds, weighed down with a heavy rock, and left for several days. To my absolute astonishment, it turned out to be the most delicious *tsukemono* I had ever tasted.

My later requests for Mother to make it with those weeds were always in vain, since her garden was once again producing cucumbers, turnips, cabbages, and nappa for *tsukemono*. She also grew Japanese eggplants, which she preserved in mustard and called mustard-*zuke*, and even raised olives for processing in lye.

Our *okazu*, or main dish, was composed mostly of vegetables and rice (a must), and the meal was always topped off with *ochazuke* and *tsukemono*. It is often said that if you had *tsukemono*, rice, and tea, that's all you'd need for a hearty meal. But as the Western cuisine began to play a greater role in our menu, the vegetable and chicken *okazu* and the vegetable and bacon *okazu* began to make way for hamburgers and sausages. Changes were slowly but surely taking place in our lifestyle, and also in our family.

Sam was entering his sophomore year and wanted a car to commute to Sacramento High, but Ben felt that Sam could attend a high school in Elk Grove, for which a bus picked up all the students in the front of their rural homes. Ben, who never had an opportunity to attend high school, insisted that wanting to go to a school in Sacramento, which was almost ten miles away and didn't have a bus service, was absolutely absurd, extravagant, and a waste of money. He rejected Sam's argument that Sacramento offered radio and electronics subjects not available at Elk Grove High.

"Almost all our neighbors are attending Elk Grove High, and whatever is good with our neighbors should be okay with you!" Ben was adamant. Ben had been forced to take over the farm when he was only sixteen years old, after Father passed on, and he did not have the option of attending even Elk Grove High.

The argument began during the grape harvesting season in a dimly lit barn with a single 75-watt bulb hanging down on a cord from the rafter above. We were packing the grapes harvested during the day, preparing them for shipment. Mother took the bundles of grapes, trimming off the unattractive fruits to pretty up each bunch, while Ben neatly packed them into wooden boxes and Sam hammered the lids onto the crates and loaded them on the truck, ready for the morning delivery to Florin's railway loading dock. They had started harvesting at sunrise, and now it was almost midnight. Everyone was tired and grouchy—a perfect environment for incubating heated exchanges of nasty and demoralizing words and phrases to release their pent-up tensions.

Initially, it was amusing; my brothers' arguments sounded sane and legit to a child of eight. I watched as the argument intensified, their voices becoming louder. They ignored Mother's frantic plea to stop. They left their work stations and began to push each other, looking for an opportunity to take a good hold of their opponent, the way they'd learned in the judo class they enrolled in during the winter season, between harvest and pruning. Ben was stockier, but Sam was taller. They both wore old white dress shirts that they intended to discard after the harvesting season, and as they grabbed each other in judo holds and flipped each other over, the shirts ripped and pieces went flying into the air. This was the first time I had ever seen an adult in a physical confrontation, and I was in total darkness as to what might happen. Worst of all, I could not root for anyone. I could not possibly take sides, since I loved them both equally.

I watched my brothers attempting to execute every judo move and strategy they had learned, swirling and scraping the dirt floor in the limited space of the barn, kicking up dust and bumping against the wall and into stacked crates. Finally, Ben appeared to be the victor, although both had lost their shirts and neither had made any overt gesture of truce. I wondered if their relationship would ever be the same.

There seemed to be tension between them from that point on, and I felt a tension in myself, for I could not favor one brother over the other. Instead, I found myself distancing from both of them, avoiding any chance of having to take sides. After the grape harvesting season, Sam packed his gear, asked Ben to take him to a bus station in Sacramento, and boarded a bus to Oakland, where our cousin lived and where he found a job as a gardener's helper.

That winter, Ben exchanged vows with Annie, a girl from Isleton, a tomato farming community about thirty miles from Florin. Since Annie had finished high school, I thought she was smart and knowledgeable and one day popped her this question: "Nay-san, where's Oz?" (Nay-san means older sister.)

"I don't know. That's just a fairy tale," she laughed.

"But it's a real place!" I was adamant and persistent because our third-grade teacher, Miss Melnor, spent a half hour every day reading several pages from the Frank L. Baum book as she sat on a stool in front of the class. She made hand gestures and facial expressions and her voice changed with each character, from the raspy witch to the timid lion. For a nine-year-old child, it was far from being a fairy tale. It was real. For twenty minutes Annie explained that I was living in a fantasy world. I was totally convinced—convinced that Annie didn't know her geography.

After the harvesting season that year, Mother left for Japan on a twenty-day voyage on the ocean liner *Tatsuta-Maru* to pay homage to Father's resting place and also to bring back my sisters, Miharu and Edith, who had been living with our aunts in Japan for the previous seven years. During Mother's absence, I was to live with Ben and Annie, who was then pregnant with their first child.

Carefree, coming and going as I pleased, it was a great life. For a few days, I felt like a hobo, but without having to worry about room and board. Yet all good things must come to end, and my time came when Ben said, "Hey, Shozo, you stink like hell. When was the last time you took a bath?" That evening, Annie scrubbed me from head to toe.

Even as a *clean* hobo, most weekends were spent with my companion, a BB air rifle, a hand-me-down from Annie's brother. I practically slept, ate, and lived with the gun, which I called Daisy, since that was the name printed on the side of the rifle. When Annie went into labor one evening, Ben rushed her to Sutter Hospital in Sacramento while I was left alone at home. At least I had the air rifle by my side to comfort and protect me, and to send me to dreamland.

It was past midnight when I suddenly woke up and saw through a curtainless window a bright, shiny object traveling across the sky from the direction of the cemetery located about half a mile southeast. Shaking and trembling, my teeth chattering, I hid deep under the *futon* and cuddled next to Daisy.

According to Japanese folklore, after a person dies the energy escapes the body in the form of a ball of fire, called *hi-no-tama*. The ball of fire, glowing in the dark and floating gently with the wind, is supposed to be about six to ten inches in diameter.

The cemetery, where local pioneer cattle ranchers were buried, was visible from our farm. I didn't know whose wandering soul it was that night, but it certainly seemed to have come to haunt me. Later, as years passed, I realized that it was a meteor, or a falling star, but still the largest I had ever seen. It came so close I could have sworn that it barely missed our house. No matter what it was, one thing is certain: I could not have survived the night without my faithful Daisy BB gun, even though it was powerless. It just went "poof!" and the BB would go "plop" and bounce off the wings of the sparrows and the robins I'd aimed at.

It was the following spring, in 1938, when Mother returned to Florin with Miharu and Edith. I was excited to "meet" my sisters for the first time (they had left when I was two), but since Miharu was eight years and Edith five years my senior, they weren't good companions for tossing balls or going fishing for catfish in a murky creek. We did, however, try to fly a kite they brought back from Japan, although with unsuccessful results. The kite was more like a top spinning in the sky before it landed with a nosedive, and yet that dismal fiasco is one of my more memorable experiences with my sisters.

* * *

A few years later, Sam exchanged vows with Kiyoko, and Miharu exchanged vows with Yosh. Sam and Kiyoko made their home in Hayward, across the bay from San Francisco, and Miharu and Yosh lived in Woodland, northwest of Sacramento and about twenty miles from Florin. Although Ben had his own family now, his household stuck close to Mother, Edith, and me.

For Miharu's union, as in all the Umemoto children's marriages except mine, Mother relied on a go-between, a *baishakunin*. Miharu's go-between was Ando-*san*, a family acquaintance from Woodland.

"Umemoto-*san*, *nagai aida gobusata itashimashita*." Ando-*san* apologized for not having kept in better touch, as Mother served tea in the parlor.

"I have good news for you," he continued in Japanese. "It's my friend Matsumoto's son, Yoshio. He is twenty-three, a Kibei Nisei (a second-generation Japanese American educated in Japan). He finished high school in Japan and is from a very good family in Wakayama Prefecture. He is a farmer but he also graduated from National School in Los Angeles, where he studied diesel engines. I think he's just the right person for your daughter, Miharu-*san*."

It did indeed seem to be a good match. Miharu was of the right age, had finished high school in Japan, and had also spent time in Wakayama. They had many things in common, including the same Wakayama Prefecture dialect. The next step in the standard procedure was for both families to write a letter to Japan to check out each other's backgrounds to ensure there weren't any sleazy skeletons lurking in their closets.

With both families' approval, Ando-*san*'s job as *baishakunin* was to set up a date for *omiai*, or a face-to-face meeting. It was the summer of 1941 when Yosh and Miharu finally met for the first time. Ando-*san* brought Yosh, with Mother and Ben acting as hosts while Miharu, Edith, and I excitedly peeked through the slit in the door left ajar to the adjoining kitchen. When Miharu whispered that Yosh was a *bidanshi*, a handsome man, we knew it was a done deal.

Miharu was called into the parlor. She behaved like a perfect, shy, and well-mannered lady, unlike the sister I knew, who never hesitated to fart in front of me.

"He's too good for her," I whispered. Edith's sharp elbow jabbed into my ribs.

They went out on a few dates.

"What did you do when you went out?" I always asked.

"Nothing," she always replied.

The wedding day arrived, with Miharu in a long, trailing wedding gown. A group picture was taken at a Japanese photo studio in Sacramento, followed by a chop suey reception dinner, where the Issei folks drank and sang to wish the newlyweds a happy and a prosperous future.

There were changes occurring all around us. Transitioning into Western culture was like coming out of the dark into a new world. There were nine Japanese students in my class, four of whom were Sansei, or third-generation Japanese Americans with Nisei parents. They all had American names—May, Florence, Carolyn, and Herbert—whereas the rest of us (except for Fred) had only our given Japanese names, which we Americanized ourselves. There was Osamu, whom we called Sam. There was Masami, who had a haircut like Mussolini, so we started to call him Mussolini, later shortening it to Moosey. There was Etsuo, who gave himself the name Eric. I wanted an American name, too. I already had a nickname, of course—Butter Ball—but wanted a more dignified moniker.

"How come you and Sam have English names and I don't?" I asked Ben, who was tinkering with the engine on our Model A Ford sedan.

"At Japanese School, I was reciting from a book and pronounced the word 'benko' instead of *benkyo* (to study) and my friends began to tease me by calling me Benko, and that's how I became Ben," he explained. I leaned on the fender as he attempted to adjust the carburetor, an occasional "shit" or "goddamn" interrupting our conversation whenever the engine began to sputter.

Ben began to talk about the builder of our Model A Ford, who didn't invent the car but invented the process of mass production. At that time, to the innocent and the naive public, he was one of the greatest heroes alive.

"I know what... We'll call you Henry, after Henry Ford," Ben suggested, and my name was instantly Henry. The following day, I proudly reported my new name to the teacher. She appeared elated to hear the news, and after she recorded it in her book, she allowed me to announce it to the class.

With pride sparkling in my eyes, I stood in front of the class and declared that my name was Henry. My friends made funny faces and the girls giggled.

"What a funny name! That's a sissy name!" they said and teased me during recess. "Oh, Henry!" my friends called me in a high-pitched girl's voice. *Butter Ball, although undignified, is better than Henry,* I thought. I began to have doubts about my new name. Walking home that day, embarrassed and ashamed, I stopped atop Bradshaw Bridge. Leaning on the rail, I stared at the creek and the adjoining pond, hoping perhaps unconsciously to drown my humiliation in the muddy waters below. The surrounding landscape was covered with green blades of barn grass dotted with patches of golden poppies, and a fresh outdoor scent filled the air, making me feel glad to be alive. Branches from stately oak trees hung over the cattail plants that flourished along the shores of the creek. From a small two-lane bridge spanning the creek, it was a scene of serene natural beauty, untouched by human hands; except for an area about thirty feet from the bridge, where it appeared as though someone may have been picnicking, not a blade of grass was bent.

"What's that?" I said when I saw on the grass a shiny black object slightly smaller than the size of a notebook. My heart began to beat faster as I approached the mystery item. It was a woman's handbag. I opened the bag, and among the woman's few personal items and driver's license was a fifty-cent silver coin. Fifty cents, or four bits, as we called it, was a substantial amount of loot for me at the time, and after fondling it for a while, I pocketed the coin, tossed the bag into the tall thicket, and continued on my way home.

With each step, however, my conscience bothered me more and more, and I began to feel miserable and sick, until finally I retreated and retrieved the purse. Putting the four bits back in the bag, I carefully placed it where I had originally found it.

After returning the coin, I was relieved, the tension was gone, and jumping in joy, I ran the rest of the way home sans the four bits. I knew I was the only one to traverse that lonely road on foot, and I was comforted the following morning on the way to school to find that the black bag was gone. The owner must have returned and retrieved her possession. But one question kept lingering in my mind: *What were they doing there?* I wondered as I looked at the flattened area of grass. *I'll bet they were making love. Yeah, that's it!*

At school, I told my friend Billy about the incident and that I thought the people were making love on the soft grass.

"They were making love, all right," he agreed. "Hey, I'll show you a place near my house where they make love all the time. How about today after school?" I accepted his invitation without a second's hesitation.

Billy was a white kid, and aside from that there was one major difference between Billy and us Japanese. Every Japanese kid in school was living on a grape farm, surrounded on all sides by vines. Billy, on the other hand, had a father with a government job at the state capitol. He lived in a sparsely populated residential region detached from the grape vineyards, with a topography conducive to a lovers' lane. The dirt road near Billy's house was nothing more than a winding tire track over the grassy terrain that led to a barren, secluded incline, remote from major roads and away from any of the farmhouses, and often pitch dark at night.

"You see those rubbers?" Billy pointed to at least a few dozen condoms scattered on the ground.

"Wow!" I was amazed and curious. I took a stick and began

examining them in detail. "Hey, Billy, you ever see them do it?"

"Sure. I saw it lots of times."

"Oh yeah? How do they do it?"

Trapped with a question he was unable to answer, he tried to change the subject. Even though neither of us had any answers, it was nevertheless a new and exciting experience worthy of sharing with other friends at school.

"You guys wanna hear something sexy?" I asked as I joined a group of boys standing by the schoolhouse waiting for the doors to open. "Hey, Billy, you're a better storyteller than me. Tell them what you showed me yesterday," I said, hoping he would go into more detail. Billy told the story in colorful detail but stopped short of explaining for what and how the condoms were used.

Still confused, I was thinking about the incident as I walked home from school that day. When I approached Bradshaw Bridge, I leaned on the rail and stared at the muddy pond and reminisced about the number of hours I'd spent fishing catfish and carp, scooping up the minnows and tadpoles, or just walking in the gooey, slippery waters. There was another deep pond nearby, under overhanging oak trees, where my neighbor Tad and I used to go fishing every weekend during the summer. We would leave our worms and fishing poles on the banks when we were done, and they would be there the following weekend, untouched, since the locale was our private fishing spot.

"It was fun when I was young," I reminisced. Now, at twelve years old going on thirteen, fishing in the pond seemed like kid stuff of bygone days. Perhaps I was at the final stretch of innocent childhood and on the verge of entering the realm of the turbulent unknown, the domain of undisciplined teenagers with sex on our minds instead of carp and catfish in a mucky millpond.

* * *

The opportunity to test the penlight came on a hike up the snow-covered Mount Baldy. There were only a few footprints in the snow, and after wondering in awe at the spectacular scenery below, I lost the trail of my own tracks and began to follow a stranger's footprints down the slope. I ended up on another path and became totally disoriented.

Comparing my hiking experience to navigating the desert, I said to myself, "I've driven tens of thousands of miles in the desert, and it's impossible to get lost. The road always leads to a town or community." This was obviously a different story. As I continued down the trail, I eventually saw cars lined up at what seemed like the parking area of a trailhead. "There! There's civilization!" I congratulated myself, but that was before I realized although I had reached civilization, I was seven miles off course, and the sun was quickly disappearing over the western horizon.

"They say you can't compare an apple with an orange," I uttered, "or a car's horsepower and mortal's foot power!" I huffed and puffed back up the mountain and finally made it to my parked truck, my penlight guiding the way in the dark.

Although I had dismally failed as a hiker, at least the penlight had passed the darkness test, and I had full confidence in it when I decided to hike up San Gorgonio Peak from the Momyer Creek trailhead a week later. According to the map, it was twenty-two miles round-trip, with a six-thousand-foot elevation gain—the equivalent to Mount Whitney, except at a lower elevation. I was all prepared with my flashlight, poncho, two pints of water and, of course, Gu and Balance brand energy food, and a couple of bologna sandwiches.

The forest ranger in a green pickup truck with an official insignia on the door was parked at the trailhead. I sprayed myself with insect repellent, belted my pouch and water bottles. When I was ready to depart, the ranger approached me.

"Going on a hike, are you?" he asked. I displayed my wilderness permit and he checked the Forest Adventure Pass I had hanging from the rearview mirror. He wished me a nice trip and warned me that it was going to be a hot day and I was going to need a lot of water. I thanked him and was on my way.

Being that this was one of the less frequently traveled trails, there were no footprints ahead of me. The area was heavily vegetated and swarming with gnats and mosquitoes, but, best of all, the path was glistening with spiderwebs lit by the morning sun, and I had to hack my way through them with both arms. This gave me a sense of hiking in true wilderness. Side trails disappeared into the gravel-strewn basins, overhanging trees formed a tunnel overhead, and oak leaves canvassed the faint trail at my feet; I felt the splendor of nature with each step.

Soon, a ranger and a companion appeared, hiking down the trail in front of me. The ranger was in his green uniform and cap, while his partner was in regular civilian hiking attire but lacking the appearance of a seasoned hiker, making me think he was an apprentice or an intern of the National Forest program.

"Here's my wilderness permit," I said, suspecting that he was patrolling the area for hikers without them.

"How far do you think you'll be going?" he asked.

"Hopefully I'm going to Dollar Lake Saddle and to San Gorgonio Peak."

"We came from the Saddle," his companion remarked. "It's beautiful up there."

"You made good time," I said. It didn't seem humanly possible to make the trek at such a pace that they'd already be coming down. Maybe I was wrong in my assessment of the hiker. *He must be a pro*, I thought.

"So, what time did you leave the trailhead?" I asked with amazement and admiration.

"Yesterday," he answered with a tone of embarrassment in his chuckle. "I went up on Vivian Creek Trail…and got lost." He laughed to shirk off his shame. He told me he had spent the night at the Saddle and the ranger was now escorting him out of the wilderness on Momyer Creek Trail. Without a heavy jacket or backpack, the man didn't seem prepared for an overnighter, and with the temperature dipping as low as the thirties up there, I was surprised he looked so well and high-spirited. As they departed, they wished me a nice, safe journey.

The morning was exceptionally hot, and at four miles from the peak I had already used the first pint of water and had less than one pint left. While I was fretting about the water situation, I noticed some seepage on the side of the mountain by the trail; water was trickling out like it was dripping from a leaky faucet. I never drank water from streams and never anticipated drinking water seeping from a mountainside, but there's always a first time. The seepage area was covered with green moss, but the water seemed clean. I collected some in my empty bottle and, after treating it with an iodine tablet, the water turned light brown and looked more like something that came out of a body rather than something that was supposed to be consumed into one. I saved the water, with the intention of waiting to drink it in a more populated trail area in case I needed help when I collapsed from poisoning.

Totally exhausted, thirsty, hungry, and sleepy, I reached the Saddle, where my route converged with South Fork Trail. A half hour's rest was a welcome treat. Usually the last stretch of any trip is the most agonizing for me, and the previous two and a half miles on South Fork Trail to San Gorgonio Peak were no exception.

There were three hikers taking the same path I was, but when our route merged with Vivian Creek Trail, it was like a super-highway, with at least thirty hikers in view. With so many hikers at the summit, it seemed safe to drink the treated water, since help was but a few steps away. I drank and waited ten minutes at the summit. Since there was no negative reaction from the water, I decided it was time to start the journey home.

It was half past three then, and since it had taken me eight hours to reach the summit, I guesstimated that it would take no longer than five hours traveling downhill. After the Vivian Creek Trail fork, the remaining eleven and a half miles to the truck was a lonely trip with not a body in sight. As the sun went down, my phobia of darkness was beginning to take its toll. The sounds of squirrels in the bushes became ghostly. The twigs on the trail appeared to be snakes. As a child, I was afraid of the dark, always fearing that some eerie creature was lurking behind me, and the phobia remained just as strong in my adult years. The wilderness that I had enjoyed and appreciated so much during daylight was now striking back with a vengeance.

It became apparent then that the glow from the penlight was inadequate on this faint wilderness path. To keep my bearings, I assumed I was on the trail as long as I could see a crag to my side, since one side of a mountain trail is usually a cliff. I stopped when I approached a grove of oak trees on level terrain that was covered with leaves and showed no sign of a path. The trail seemed to have suddenly disappeared. I went for my bottle of water, since I was perspiring, but to my astonishment, the water was ice cold, and I noticed then that the air was nippy, making me wonder if I was sweating from fear rather than from heat.

"Don't panic! Freeze! Calm down! Relax! Don't move!" I kept repeating to myself. I marked my spot with a cross, stuck a twig in the ground, and proceeded straight ahead. "One, two, three," I counted the steps so I could return to the same spot if I didn't find the trail and had to start my search anew. "Twenty one, twenty two…" and there appeared a continuation of the path. The trail became more distinct the lower the elevation, but then rock and boulder fields interrupted my way and suddenly I was in the middle of a large dry riverbed covered with stones and not the slightest hint of a trail. The penlight was casting a ray only several yards ahead and was absolutely useless for trailblazing in the moonless night in the forest with just the dim glow of starlight. I backtracked onto the trail and, marking the spot with a small pile of rocks hikers call a "duck," I proceeded straight ahead, counting my steps.

"…fifteen, sixteen…" I constantly looked to both sides in search of the trail. I finally noticed an outline of a familiar rock formation across the wash, and suspected the trail resumed nearby. I was right.

Back on the trail again, I forged ahead, and when I heard the sound of rushing water in the distance, I knew that all was well, since I had parked my truck across the stream. Flashing the tiny beam of light into the waters, I saw five large rocks, with one huge white rock smack in the middle. "Lucky for me! I'd sure hate to wade through the water. It must be freezing!" I shouted as I hopped on the rocks, but *splash!* The huge white rock in the middle had been just an illusion in the dark. Instead of a stepping-stone, it was a patch of white sand on the bottom of an icy stream bed, three feet deep.

The rock was only an illusion, but the icy water that saturated my pants and drenched my shoes was no trick, and I began to shiver as I hurried up to the truck parked several hundred yards away. I always kept an extra pair of shoes and socks inside. I turned on the truck heater full blast, dried my feet, and sat in my drenched pants until I stopped trembling. I drove home with the illusion of that white boulder in the middle of the stream vividly emblazoned on my mind.

* * *

My brothers and sisters were getting married and starting their own families. The country was emerging from the depression and entering prosperous times. Grapes and strawberry prices were rising, and the future could only be described as bright, if not dazzling. Or could this also have been just an illusion? An embargo was imposed on Japan in the summer of 1941, freezing all Japanese assets in the United States. Mother's life savings in Sumitomo Bank and Shokin Ginko eventually became worthless, but the worst was yet to come five months later. Pearl Harbor.

Chapter Five

"BECAUSE WE'RE JAPS, THAT'S HOW COME"

I was driving in the desert toward the Chuckwalla Mountains, just south of Joshua Tree National Monument across Interstate 10 and between Indio and the Arizona border. Mining activities in the area spanned from the 1870s to the 1940s, piquing my fascination with both the forty-niners and recreational gold prospecting. I planned to spend a day or two basking in the desert sun and probing for nuggets the old-timers may have left behind. I had spent a small fortune on Fisher Gold Bug and Minelab detectors, a gasoline-powered dry washer to separate gold from dirt, and a gas-powered dredge for prospecting in the mountain streams, but I had yet to collect even a pennyweight of gold.

A psychiatrist may call it rationalization, but the reward from recreational gold prospecting is not amassing riches but nourishing the ever flickering hope of discovering a nugget, coupled with enjoying nature in its prime—almost always in a tranquil area undisturbed by civilization. Members of the Gold Prospectors Association of America (like I am) also have the perk of being allowed to prospect on the association's gold claims. On this trip to the remote desert, I chose the Busty Steve, Red Cloud, and Bumper Cactus claims, perhaps because I was attracted to their cool-sounding names.

From where I lived, it would take several hours to drive to the area, and many more hours to locate the claims. Initially locating a particular mining claim is an extremely difficult task, even with the aid of coordinates and modern GPS gadgets. Before affordable GPS systems were available, I once spent two whole days trying to find a single claim, since there were certainly no road or trail signs, and in that case not even a landmark. With this in mind, I decided to spend the night camping adjacent to Interstate 10, near Joshua Tree National Monument in a BLM (Bureau of Land Management) camping area a short distance from Chuckwalla. I could then have an early morning start and spend the whole day locating the claim if I needed to.

By sunrise the following morning, I was driving on a dirt road toward the Bumper Cactus claim. Abandoned mining structures dotted the landscape along the barren desert as I rambled over a dusty, narrow road, with not another living soul in sight. This journey would transport anyone into a world of yore, when life seemed less complicated and nature was in its full, undisturbed beauty and grandeur. Chuckwalla definitely had the aura of my birthplace of Florin, where some structures from the pre-World War II era remain, now in their final stages of decay.

* * *

Florin was our home, where we laughed and played, and I thought that glee would last forever. Was that also an illusion? Little did we know at the time that someday we would have to bid farewell to our friends and neighbors—never to return again—and Florin would be just a fragment of memory that would fade and maybe someday disappear.

Was it also an illusion to believe that we had equal rights as

American citizens? Immediately after Pearl Harbor, the home of our neighbor Mr. Ito was ransacked, and the FBI took him into custody with two thousand other Japanese, who were later sent to internment camps primarily because they were important and respected leaders in their communities. That Mr. Ito had served in the United States Army during World War I (and that the upper part of his nose was missing from when a bullet had nearly taken his life) was apparently not considered by government officials.

Rumors began to proliferate that our homes would be searched, too. Edith torched her entire collection of magazine clippings of Emperor Hirohito and his relatives, as well as any Japanese magazines we had in the house. Then the rumor spread that we would have to leave the West Coast entirely. Nobody knew when, by what means, or for how long. Beyond today, our future was an unknown entity.

In March of 1942, the U.S. military issued Exclusion Order Number 1, ordering everyone of Japanese ancestry to vacate Bainbridge Island, off the coast of Washington state. Approximately 350 residents left and arrived at the Manzanar relocation camp on April 1, occupying Block 3. This was soon followed by Exclusion Order Number 2, which was directed at Terminal Island (off the coast of Southern California), whose residents arrived at Manzanar on April 2. We knew then that we too would be forced to leave our homes, but we did not have the faintest clue as to when or where we would go. Days passed, and days turned into weeks. It was the end of April, and there was still no order for evacuation in the Florin area. We started to hear rumors that those of us residing in Central Valley would not have to evacuate.

Despite this optimistic speculation, however, we began to prepare ourselves for departure just the same. Ben made arrangements with a shipper who handled our crop to look after the farm while we were away. He also asked our friend and neighbor Mr. Barnby to store our car and furniture on his property, as well as keep an eye on our land.

I helped Ben gather some flat boards from the back of our barn and garage so he could cut them into sizes that would be suitable for boarding up our windows.

"How come we gotta leave this place?" I asked Ben.

"Get me that board," he ordered, apparently buying time to mull over the question, since he was probably wondering about that himself. As anti-Japanese sentiment became stronger with each passing day, we heard ourselves described as "Japs" in the media. In their eyes, we were just as responsible for the war as the ones who had bombed Pearl Harbor.

After a long hesitation, Ben answered with a tone of disgust and anger, "Because we're Japs, that's how come." An afterthought he added, "We're dangerous," and laughed at his sarcasm. With all the Japanese community leaders removed by the FBI, a ban on community meetings and general assembly, and a five-mile travel restriction, not to mention the substantial number of Nisei serving in the armed forces of this country, how could there be even a remote chance of threat or sabotage?

Finally, in mid-May, Exclusion Order Number 92—a compulsory evacuation order—was tacked on to a power line pole bordering Bradshaw Road in front of our vineyard. It designated a perimeter around Florin that included about 1,500 Japanese residents and decreed that the area must be evacuated by midnight on May 30, 1942. It also designated a location for the head of the family to register.

Ben, representing our family, went to register as directed on the poster. He was told we had a choice of moving east, to Wyoming, for example, or being sent to the Fresno Assembly Center, which had been set up to receive thousands of evacuees just like us. Five thousand Japanese and Japanese Americans on the West

Coast had already voluntarily moved away from their homes and into the interior regions, where they lived with relatives, but for us that was not an option, since we didn't know anyone in America who wasn't on the coast.

"What's an assembly center?" Ben asked the registrar, who explained it was a temporary facility that would hold evacuees before they were sent to one of the ten permanent camps then in various stages of construction.

"When and where?" Ben wanted to know because Annie was four months pregnant with their second child.

"We don't have a clue," the man answered.

After explaining Annie's situation, Ben was given the choice of going to the nearby Fresno Assembly Center or directly to Manzanar, a permanent camp located east of the Sierra, in the Owens Valley desert of California. Under Exclusion Order Number 92, 350 people were already being sent to Manzanar, and more were destined for the Fresno and Pinedale Assembly Centers. The majority of my friends were being sent to the Fresno Assembly Center.

None of the options sounded appealing, of course, but Manzanar seemed to Ben to be the wisest choice considering Annie's condition. At least she wouldn't have to travel a second time during her pregnancy. It turned out to be a good decision in the end, since the people we knew who went to the Fresno Assembly Center were transferred to the Jerome Relocation Center in Arkansas several months later, and, shortly thereafter, when Jerome was closed because it was operating below capacity, they were transferred again, to Rohwer Relocation Center in Arkansas.

Ben returned home from registering and informed us that we were going to Manzanar.

We were assigned Family Number 8648 and ordered to report to the Elk Grove railroad station on Sunday, May 24. At age thirteen, I was more concerned about being separated from my friends than anything else. When you're a teenager, your friends are your universe. I also didn't know at the time why most of my Japanese classmates were leaving for the Fresno Assembly Center, and the rest for the Pinedale Assembly Center, but no one seemed to be going to Manzanar. My only consolation was that Sierra School, which had predominantly Japanese students, closed early in May, in preparation for the evacuation.

As exclusion posters went up in the area, bargain hunters began to canvass the vicinity, offering to buy appliances, cars, and furniture at a fraction of their costs. Two men came in a sedan, and while one sat in the car motionless and mum, the driver approached us and began to talk about the good deal he could make us ("unlike the others"), on purchasing our refrigerator and washing machine, kindly offering us a free estimate on our appliances. When everyone went into the house to talk things over, the man who had stayed behind in the car got out and began roaming our yard, barn, and garage, looking for something of value.

Shortly after they left, buying nothing, Ben contemplated, "You know, I thought I heard a noise...something like our chain hoist." Sure enough, it had disappeared, along with wrenches and carpentry tools. Ben added, "You know, those guys came in a sedan. How did they expect to carry a refrigerator in a sedan? They had no intention of buying the refrigerator or the washing machine!" He was furious. The anger in his voice was mixed with disgust at himself for not having detected their obvious intentions.

Thereafter, we kept our eyes on all the strangers who came on our property, but when a couple of my schoolmates visited me and wanted my old bicycle, they didn't even try to bargain, they just took my bicycle and ran. The following day, when I called on Gene, one of the culprits, he pointed a .22 caliber rifle straight into my chest and suggested that I leave, a request to which I graciously complied. I was pretty sure he was bluffing, but since his family had an unscrupulous reputation, and since his finger was on the trigger, I wasn't about to call his bluff.

At the end of May, Mother announced, "Your bag is ready and you can start packing." She had made something similar in size and shape to an army duffel bag for every member of the family by bleaching old cotton sacks from Blue Rose rice and sulfur dusting powder. I was already wearing the only shoes and jacket I owned, so what remained to be packed were underwear, a few shirts, a pair of trousers, and some personal odds and ends. A good portion of my bag was empty.

Shortly after the outbreak of war, all "contraband" had been confiscated, including our Kodak Brownie cameras, our 12-gauge shotgun, and our .22 caliber rifle, but hidden under the bedroom floor was a samurai sword and a short sword that was traditionally worn under a woman's wide obi sash. The samurai sword was definitely too long to take, but the woman's sword could be concealed in the bag among my clothing. My dream of bringing the weapon was shattered, however, when Mother saw me fondling the sword and guessed my sneaky intention. Mother reprimanded me and continued to lecture that disobeying the rules would bring disgrace to the entire family as well as to all the Japanese. Yet holding a sword had always given me a feeling of adventure and an imaginary sense of power that I was reluctant to relinquish. I dismantled the sword in secrecy and, throwing the blade in the crawl space under the house, I snuck a part of the sword's handle, called a *fusa* (guard), in my duffel bag.

Things of value were packed into two steamer trunks and left in a federal storage facility, some furniture was sent to Mr. Barnby, and the remaining items were left in the house and the barn.

There was one particular piece of outdoor furniture that held sentimental value: the *suzumen*. Although it had outlasted

Father, years of winter rain and sizzling summer heat had taken their toll; the boards were warped, the nails were rusted and loose, and the legs were beginning to wobble and sway. It was evident that the *suzumen* was at its journey's end. The wood platform had turned black with years of weathering, some of the boards were cracked, and the once sturdy and solid struc-ture was now leaning toward its final resting place. Beneath the crumbling *suzumen* were cucumber sprouts from seeds that had fallen through the cracks the previous autumn. Now protected by the wood slab in its final days, their future was unknown. We would not be there to witness whether they would produce a new plant or wither and turn to dust.

Their future was just as uncertain as mine. I would never again be able to sit on the *suzumen* and listen to Mother's sto-ries under the clear, star-filled skies and the bright gray moon. I'd never be able to taste the fresh vegetables grown from the seeds the *suzumen* had dried, and never be able to crunch on the white dried persimmons while playing Chinese checkers in the cold and rainy winter evenings with just a hibachi to keep us warm. The day had arrived to say *sayonara* to the wide wooden bench, to depart from my birthplace for a remote, isolated, and unknown place that had a strange sounding name, "Manzanar," and held an uncertain destiny.

Mother covered the *tsukemono* vats with cheesecloth to keep the flies and the insects away before nailing down the door.

"When are we coming back?" I asked. And then with a teen-age sarcasm I added with a laugh, "We'll be eating rotten *tsuke-mono!*" I now deeply regret uttering that remark. Mother simply ignored my comment and continued with her chores.

This was the last time she would ever see the home she had devoted thirty years of her life to building through sweat and toil. As she covered the vats of *tsukemono* that day, did she have even a faint glimmer of hope that she would return soon? Perhaps in a matter of a few weeks? Or did she know deep in her heart that she'd never be able to come back, and in her chores was making a final tribute, saying goodbye to the vats of *tsukemono* that had brought so much satisfaction and joy to her family for so many years. Was she, in her special way, laying them to rest?

Those vats of *tsukemono* are long gone, but the memory and tradition lingers on, and after each evening meal I still have to have my *ochazuke* and *tsukemono*. Occasionally I even crave for that *tsukemono* made from the weeds with mustard-colored flowers.

Finally all the windows were boarded up, doors were nailed shut, farm equipment was corralled into the barn, mattresses were covered with worn and torn sheets, and kitchen cabinets were emptied save for a few cups, dishes, and *chawan* (rice bowls).

Mother stared at the chiming wall clock with its brass pendulum swinging from side to side. She took a key with a butterfly handle and stuck it through the hole in the face of the clock and wound it several clicks at a time.

"How come you're winding the clock?" I asked. She didn't answer but just stood and watched the pendulum swing. Perhaps she only did it because that's what she had done for the past thirty years, twenty of it with her late husband.

"When will we come home? One week? One month? Maybe one year? Two years? Three years?" She did not reply, for no one knew.

Mother opened the gate to the chicken coop and left out a few trays of water and scattered feed all over the yard for the chickens. Under the faucet she left another pan for water to drip into for as long as our five-thousand-gallon water tank would last.

Then she kicked down the fence post and flattened the chicken wire fence so the chickens and jackrabbits could help themselves to her vegetable garden, which had fed the family for thirty years and, she hoped, might feed the remaining residents for several more months.

She took a good final look at the trunk of the dead willow tree lying flat on its side with snow white mushrooms sprouting from the decaying bark, the beginning of new life. Perhaps it reminded her of the prosperous times, or perhaps the hard times, or perhaps her husband, who had planted the once graceful weeping willow whose sagging branches swayed with the wind.

As I strolled through the house for the last time, I heard the ticktock of the clock. Watching the swinging pendulum, I said, "I'll see you tomorrow." Once outside, I said to our boarded-up home, "This is goodbye…forever."

I took a handful of four-penny nails and hammered the initials "HU" into the young sycamore tree by the empty trough that had once watered the two horses that plowed the land. I hoped that at least this tree would still be standing when we returned one day. Years later, I would discover that it had wilted and turned to dust, just as my life in Florin had become but a memory.

* * *

I continued down the road in the Chuckwalla Mountains, and it was easy sailing except for the dust and bumps and the couple of ravines where I had to stop, get out, and step down on the dry creek bed to make sure the sand was compacted enough to be passable. I vowed to bring my four-wheel-drive truck on the next excursion, which would make me feel a lot more secure.

Locating the claim, I parked along a hillside sheltered by large boulders, an ideal spot for spending a night or two. After a light lunch, I attached my Garmin GPS to my belt (and my Garmin Foretex GPS to my wrist as a backup) and walked to a clearing to tune my Minelab gold detector. When it was ready, I tested it on the ground, and I was soon carried away, walking freely, poking here and there, and slowly inching away from the truck until I had gone so far astray that the truck was nowhere in sight.

"Better get back to the truck and get everything set up for an afternoon of prospecting," I said, and walked toward the truck, which was supposedly behind the hill…but, I soon found out, the wrong hill. I looked around and suddenly realized that the area was dotted with dozens of small hills, each the size of a football field and ranging from about one hundred to two hundred feet in elevation. They all looked alike. I consulted my GPS units, but they were turned off; the last waypoint recorded was the city of Gardena. Without the location of the truck entered into the GPS units, both of the high-tech instruments were totally useless.

"It must be the next hill," I said, and walked around it only to find that it must be the *next* one. This continued hill after hill until I finally came up with a new plan.

"Why not climb to the top of the hill, where surely I'll be able to see the truck?" I confidently hiked up the closest hill with the expectation of spotting my truck immediately, but the bright idea turned out to be a dud, since all I could see from the top was an array of almost identical hills; the truck was probably hidden behind one of them. I made several more attempts on other hills and finally scrapped the plan altogether.

I felt a cool breeze and, looking at my watch, saw it was already past three o'clock. I had no water, was wearing only a T-shirt, and it was February, which meant there were only a couple hours of daylight left. Without a flashlight, mobility becomes nil in this area flourishing with cholla cactus, also called the jumping cholla, because its thorns cling to, and keep clinging to, whatever they touch. In the dark, there's no avoiding them. I'd already had experience using long-nose pliers to remove the spines with their microscopic barbs from my arms and legs, and I was in no mood to repeat that.

I felt my heart pounding a little faster.

"Calm down! Better not panic!" I kept mumbling to myself. "Don't move, keep cool, think things out, plan out what to do so you don't make a fatal decision."

Standing dazed in the barren Chuckwalla desert, after a while I finally felt I had arrived at a sane decision in regards to surviving this unwelcome predicament; I would concentrate on finding shelter.

"I gotta find a place to spend the night," I said and began looking for a large boulder or a cave, or any kind of shelter, but to no avail. The rocks sprinkling the area were all too small.

When I realized that I likely wouldn't survive the night without shelter, I became frantic. The clock was ticking away, and in desperation I began to look for a nice flat rock that would be visible from the air. I needed a large, level surface to rest on so a helicopter would be able to spot my dead body quickly and easily, should it come to that.

After a short search, I found a rock just large enough to sit on, placed my Minelab gold detector on the ground, and relaxed, trying to compose myself. I looked around and noticed that I hadn't seen a single lizard or snake, or even ants, which I usually run into on my trips. It was strange, cold, and lonely, like a prelude to my death. The late afternoon sun was beginning to cast a pink glow over the western horizon.

I stared into the desert. This was the first time ever in my life that I had searched for a place to lie down and die.

As I continued searching for a shelter, cave, or deathbed, whichever appeared first, I watched the sun go down as the temperature kept sinking and I began to shiver. I had practically given up on finding my truck. I was at the edge of insanity, dazed and groggy, when suddenly and miraculously, my feet were on a smooth surface. I was a dirt road! I could hardly believe it when I noticed a set of tire marks—my tire marks!—and that was all I needed to guide me back to the truck.

This experience of hopelessly wandering around for hours in the desert, like a derelict at sea, reminded me of a family heirloom, the Verona Clipper.

* * *

The Verona Clipper was a pair of bookends shaped like two halves of a sailing ship. Father had bought it, and although it was abandoned many times over the years, it always found its way home.

The Clipper had its origin in the Verona Copper Foundry in Illinois. A stack of ingot lay on the floor, ready to be cast, but what would it become? Would it be loved and treasured and travel the continents and across the vast seas, or lie in someone's attic to be forgotten? The day finally arrived when it was cast into bookends, taking the shape of a clipper ship, and destined to be sent across the country to Sacramento, California, where it rested on the corner shelf of the Yorozu Dry Goods store. People looked, fingered the glistening copper surface, tapped and listened to the solid tone of the shiny metal. After learning the price, they always replaced it on the shelf.

"Umemoto-*san*, how was the crop this year?" the storekeeper asked Father during one of my parents' shopping excursions.

"Very good. With the war in Europe, the prices were high. With the vines at their prime, we shipped more grapes than ever before."

Mother picked up the Verona Clipper.

"Papa, why don't you get that for your desk?" Mother always had an affinity for knickknacks.

So the Verona Clipper now had a home. Father placed his cloth-covered sky blue ledger book between the bookends and sighed. "We put some money in Shokin Ginko and Sumitomo Bank and still have enough left over to send to my brother for safekeeping in case we ever return to Japan. The money in the banks is for our sons—their education and their future."

World War I was ending and the Roaring Twenties were about to begin. The economy was booming, and the Verona Clipper embraced the prosperous records of our farm's activities. It cradled the records of the new addition built onto the house; it kept the plans and expenses of installing a new water pump to irrigate the vineyard and the five-thousand-gallon water tank to bring running water into the house. It secured the documents for the new Model T Ford as well as the new building to house the migrant Filipino workers hired during the grape harvesting season. With the economy in full motion and everything going so well, Papa was surely intending to make this a permanent home for his young family, and for the Verona Clipper, for years and generations to come.

Suddenly, the seemingly everlasting prosperous America came to an abrupt end with the Crash of '29, and two years later, a tragedy struck the family with the passing of Father. The Verona Clipper, now tarnished in spots, was moved to the bottom of a trunk, to make its voyage to Japan with Mother and her five children. The Clipper, once holding the golden dreams of a flourishing immigrant, was now empty. Even more depressing was when Mother found out that the thousands of dollars sent for safekeeping to Father's brother in Japan was gone. Gone, since he had spent every cent of it to run for and then hold office as the governor of Wakayama Prefecture.

Once the official mourning period was over and Mother had been recuperated for her monetary losses, the Verona Clipper was again stowed away at the bottom of the trunk for the three-week voyage back to America. Returned to Florin, it was again placed on the desk that had once promised so much, so many dreams of the bright future. Now, instead of holding together Father's ledgers, it held books for the home study course Ben was pursuing, since at sixteen he was taking over the farm and was unable to continue with his high school education.

By 1939, the economy was gaining upward momentum and it was time for Ben to put a down payment on twenty acres of land adjacent to our farm. The ledger reassumed its position between the Verona Clipper bookends, keeping records of the strawberry crops and young grape saplings maturing into vines. With better times ahead, the Verona Clipper was ready to embrace the records of prosperity for the second time.

But soon the United States was at war with Japan, which was followed by the evacuation of Japanese from the West Coast, and the Verona Clipper was placed at the bottom of the steamer trunk for the third time. The family savings vanished and we were forced to abandon the farm it took two generations to build. The Verona Clipper had nothing to embrace. It too was being abandoned, its destiny unknown. For Ben, who had spent ten of his best years toiling on the land while his friends were attending school and playing baseball on weekends, he had nothing to show for his labor but calluses on his hands. This too was Ben's last farewell, for he neither saw the farm nor the Verona Clipper again.

The Verona Clipper lay at the bottom of a trunk at a lonely federal storage facility in Sacramento, with nothing to embrace but the memories of the past two generations and empty dreams of the future. Would it find its way home and eventually support another new beginning? Or would it slowly sink to the bottom of a deep chasm full of empty promises, never to surface again?

Chapter Six

HELLO, MANZANAR

Presto Prints was the name of my printing firm, a small shop with four employees. Occasionally we'd have slack periods when we'd twiddle our thumbs while waiting for a job to trickle in, and during one of these lulls, Daniel, one of the employees who did bindery work and deliveries for the shop, decided to thoroughly clean the concrete floor with soap and water. He had just finished scrubbing the area outside the bathroom when I dashed across it and made a quick left turn. When I pivoted on my foot, I slipped on the soapy film, flew through the air, and headed for the solid concrete floor. Thump! I landed on my left hip and left elbow, harder than I had ever fallen in my entire life. To my astonishment, I survived without a fracture, not even a bruise, although I felt nauseated for the next forty-five minutes. Soon after, something happened to my self-assurance. I began to harbor a feeling of invincibility, and perhaps that was what made me decide to climb Mount Baldy when moderate to heavy rain was forecast for that day.

It was late autumn with a freezing morning temperature of thirty degrees at the Ski Hut trailhead. Since there were no cars at the parking area, I assumed there were no others on the trail. I sat in the car for a moment, having serious doubts about climbing Mount Baldy in such severe weather, but I finally said, "After all, I'm invincible," and started up the trail. It never occurred to me that I was already at 5,500 feet and would climb another 4,500 feet to the summit, where it would be even colder. Added to that the windchill factor would make the temperature feel even lower. I had a thermometer hanging from my backpack strap, and it wasn't long before I saw the mercury drop to twenty degrees. Snowflakes floated in the air.

"Nice to know there's other crazy people," said a voice, appearing to have come out of nowhere. It was a hiker behind me. I stopped and stepped aside to let him pass. Later, two other hikers overtook me. Being a slow climber, I was left behind, but the knowledge that I had company somewhere out there on the trail was reassuring, and things didn't appear as bleak then as when I was alone. There's always comfort in numbers.

* * *

In 1942, 113,000 West Coasters were ordered to evacuate their homes, and 10,000 of us were sent to Manzanar, an unfamiliar place that wasn't even on most maps. My family arrived at camp on a beautiful spring morning, the dazzling Mount Williamson in the background still capped with snow. The dry air with a touch of sagebrush scent from the surrounding desert was fresh, invigorating, and soothing—until we entered our assigned room in a tarpapered barrack.

There were six of us—Mother, Edith, Ben and Annie with their son Ronny, and me—all sharing a twenty-by-twenty-five-foot space. The four rooms in the barrack were separated by a single sheet of plywood. The group in the room next to ours was a family of nine: seven children and their parents. When the adults were away, the children often stood on each other's shoulders and hung onto the top of the partition, poking their heads over like a bunch of Kilroys, spooking us at the least expected moments.

Ben strung a length of twine across the room and Mother hung the sheets that she had brought in her duffel bag, separating our room in two. On one side was Ben's family, and on the other, Mother, Edith, and me.

Griffith Company, a construction firm from Los Angeles, built the original structures occupied by evacuees, and later the Nisei evacuee construction team swept through the camp updating these minimal shells, installing linoleum and plasterboard to cover the floors, walls, and ceilings. After that, to our great relief, those little Kilroys bothered us no more.

Our family was still intact, but we no longer sat at the same dining table and talked about the day's happenings. That daily time in which we comforted, supported, and encouraged each other was a thing of the past. Although Ben's family sat together at the mess hall, Mother, who worked there, ate with her fellow employees before opening the doors to the rest of the evacuees. Edith sat with her best friend, Grace, while I dined with my friend from our former neighborhood, Frank.

In late autumn, Ben and Annie welcomed the latest addition to their family—Janice—at Manzanar Hospital, within the camp's barbed wire.

Starting in February of the following year, the indefinite leave program allowed some internees to move away from Manzanar for lives in interior agricultural regions and Midwestern urban areas. Vacancies began to surface in our block, and crowded families claimed the additional living space.

"We're moving," Ben informed me one day. "We'll be going to Barrack 8 and you'll be going to Barrack 14." The news was unexpected, but it seemed like an excellent idea, since that would allow the family next door to cut a doorway in the partition and double the living quarters for those seven kids. It was also great for us, since Ben's growing family could now have extra space and privacy as well.

Initially, Barrack 14 was reserved as a community service building that could be used for preschool or arts and crafts class-rooms, but since the additional space wasn't needed for those purposes, Barrack 14 was redesignated as a residential barrack.

"It's a brand new room!" I said when I entered our new abode.

"Yes, Dusty but nice," Mother agreed.

"The next room is vacant. I wonder who our new neighbor's gonna be," Edith commented. That room remained vacant until the day we left the camp.

I often wondered why Ben and Annie didn't move next door. Ben's barrack was located at the eastern end of the block, while we were in the last barrack on the western edge. He and his family never came to visit us, and vice versa. I never stepped into their room, and neither did Mother or Edith. It would have been nice if they were in the next room, all of us living as one happy family. I often wondered who made the choice to live at opposite ends of the block when there was an obvious alternative, but to this day I do not have the answer. In hindsight, I often wonder why I never visited them myself.

Mother attended Seicho-no-Ie meetings (similar in concept to Christian Science practice) and Edith was preoccupied with her violin and *shigin* (Japanese classical singing) lessons and sewing classes, in addition to her job at Manzanar's clothing factory. Edith had her interests and friends, and I had mine; we hardly ever participated in activities together or discussed our joys and sadnesses the way other siblings do, even though we lived in the same room for over three years.

Perhaps one of the greatest tragedies arising from our evacuation and internment at camp was not the material loss but the profound damage to our family bond, once so pristine, so tender and so warm. Before Manzanar, I never doubted the resilience of our family unity, but I came to discover how wrong I had been.

A few months after arriving at Manzanar, the school term started. Invariably, in the early afternoon, the northerly wind invaded camp, turning loose sand into a penetrating dust storm. The fine granules erupted like brown volcanic ash and blew through the crevices in the wooden floor. As our teacher lectured, we took notes while constantly brushing sand off our notebooks. By sundown, the wind would almost instantly turn into a cool gentle breeze, dying away as suddenly as it had arisen.

During the early days at Manzanar High School, our classrooms were poorly outfitted; we did not even have chairs or desks. In time, the furniture arrived, and textbooks to boot, followed by installation of linoleum floors and plasterboard on the wall.

A classroom without chairs, students without textbooks, a room filled with sand and dust—that was the early days of Manzanar High School. Classes continued nevertheless, and we constantly improvised around the voids. Before we had chairs, we sat on the floor and leaned against the wall. Without text books, we gave oral reports and participated in discussions. One early lesson that wedged in my mind was about an airplane that flew straight up into the sky.

There's an airplane that goes straight up in the air? How can that be? I thought to myself.

"That's called an autogyro," one of the other students explained. Some of my classmates knew about these gyroplanes, which had a couple of giant blades swirling on an overhead propeller, but Rok, whom I met in class and who later became my lifelong friend, was the only one who knew about helicopters. We had never heard of helicopters.

"Perhaps Rokuro could give a talk next week," our teacher, Mr. Greenlee, suggested.

Rok's presentation of Igor Sikorsky's invention was indeed a rare treat in more ways than one. We sat and listened to Rok's interesting talk and had no homework for the day.

I was fascinated by airplanes. Before World War II, I often watched the North American AT-6s fly over our barn from nearby Mather Field. Our property must have been their landmark, since the planes always swept over the barn and made a wide 180-degree turn over our vineyard.

Since I was interested in airplanes, I didn't hesitate when my friend Wanger suggested we visit Rok's barrack to see his model airplanes. Wanger had heard from their mutual friend that Rok was an avid model plane builder.

I had never seen any barrack room like Rok's. His ceiling was hung with countless model airplanes—mostly fighter planes, including the German Messerschmitt, the British Spitfire, the American Lightning, and of course, the Japanese Zero. Rokuro knew what octane gasoline each one required, and what horsepower and kind of engine powered the aircraft. These were not plastic models but figures made from balsa wood. He cut out the pieces, glued them together, covered them with paper, and doped (lacquered) them, all of which required an amount of patience I thought contrary to his usual temperament. I certainly would not have the diligence or skill to imitate his work, but I thought I would try making my own model plane out of scrap pine lumber. I completely failed in my attempt, since the plane got smaller each time I made a correction, finally resulting in a tiny figure with a wing span of only three inches.

Instead of making models, I resigned myself to just looking at pictures of fighter planes. One day I heard the sound of some single-engine aircrafts coming from the direction of Highway 395, only several hundred yards from our block. I ran toward the airstrip along the eastern sector of the camp and there spotted what appeared to be a squadron of P-51s.

P-51s were the "fighter" or "pursuit" planes built by North

American Aviation. First designed for the British Royal Air Force, the P-51s were only picked up by the U.S. Air Force in the spring of 1943, but I recognized them by their low wings tapered to square tips.

The P-51s were on some form of tactical training maneuver, and for the next several weeks they landed and took off daily on the asphalt runway near camp. Then, abruptly, they were gone, and for the remainder of our stay the only thing I saw soaring over the lonely deserted airstrip were blackbirds and sparrows. *Why was Manzanar developed so close to the strip? What was the mission of those P-51 fighter planes?* I pondered these questions during the war years, but nobody seemed to know the answer at the time.

Decades later, I covered the area with my metal detector, hoping to uncover some clues to these mysteries. I walked and drove on the asphalt runway a dozen times or more. The airstrip, hidden behind sagebrush only several hundred feet from the highway, remained undetected by thousands of motorists passing by every day. It was many years later that I learned the airfield had been built in 1941 to test Army Air Force bombers, but for some reason it was never fully utilized.

More recently, as I stood on the very ground I called home for three years, I watched the setting sun cast shadows on the Inyo Mountains and recalled the swoosh of the props and the purr of the Allison engine as a sleek, slender phantom fuselage touched down among the tumbling tumbleweeds over the runway behind the heavy outgrowth of sagebrush.

I looked around at what had been Manzanar—Manzanar, a city of ten thousand strong, born in 1942 and disappearing abruptly in 1945, a desert community with many faces, and many ideals, taking with it the gloom and despair as well as a spirit of pride, joy, laughter. Manzanar, like the mysterious P-51 Mustangs that had suddenly appeared from the sky one day and then disappeared just as magically into the blue yonder, now remains silent in the desert sands, still harboring many secrets that no one can ever unveil.

* * *

The temperature began to drop and the gust of wind that swept across the mountainside was now hurling snow against my body without mercy as I continued to follow the boot imprints another hiker had left in the snow-covered trail. I was cold, but the white mountainscape was becoming even more magnificent with each gust. Growing up in the Central Valley of California, snow was nonexistent, and whenever I saw scenery on Christmas cards, I felt envious of the people who were able to play in such a winter wonderland. It was at Manzanar that this boyhood dream finally came true.

* * *

One midwinter morning when I peered out the barrack window, the rooftops were covered with snow and the granite of Mount Williamson to the west was painted white, with sprinklings of dark green conifers. The Inyo Mountains to the east and the Alabama Hills to the south appeared as though a smooth blanket of cotton had rolled across the untamed terrain. Disappearing into the northern horizon were the snow-covered ridges of the ragged Sierra Nevada.

It was a sight to behold, but without proper attire (which no one owned in Manzanar at that time), it was too cold to truly enjoy the snow. By early afternoon, however, the cloudless skies and the warm winter sun made it ideal for some outdoor play. Perfect…except it was a school day.

"Hank, have you noticed the scenery?" Mas, my classmate, spread his arms like an eagle, turned his palms up, and rotated slowly as he took in every bit of his surroundings, as if this were his last moment on earth. "This is paradise! This must be heaven!" He was absolutely correct. It was by any estimation a heavenly grandeur.

"This is only going to last a few more hours," he hinted. "School? We have a whole semester of classes ahead of us," he pressed the point.

It didn't take much until I was convinced that our winter dreamland was too good to waste by attending classes.

"Hey, you wanna ditch school?" I asked.

"Well, okay, but remember, you suggested it, not me."

We chose a firebreak area far from school, adjacent to Block 28, where Mas lived. A firebreak is basically a vacant area without any flammable structures, kept that way to "break" or deter fire from spreading onto other structures. Between each cluster of four blocks was a firebreak at least 420 feet wide. Each block was self-sustainable, with a mess hall, toilet, and laundry facilities able to accommodate its three hundred residents. The firebreak was an ideal area to play and enjoy the wonderful and beautiful surprise of snow. The area was empty, as though we were the only two individuals in Manzanar. It was paradise in our desert home. We enjoyed our play as long as we could, but eventually our bare hands became numb and our street shoes were soaking wet and our toes had lost all feeling. It was time to end our escapade.

We scurried to the Block 28 recreation room, and after a minute of fumbling at the door latch with our numbed fingers, we were finally out of the cold. We lit the oil-burning heater, but it was not enough to stop us from shivering. We wondered if ditching school and playing outdoors in the snow had been such a smart idea after all. Furthermore, cutting classes was unheard of in camp. But since we had already broken one rule, Mas suggested that perhaps we could break another one by filling ourselves with some spirit to warm our bodies from the inside and, at the same time, drown out our feelings of guilt.

"Gandhi, who lives in the next barrack, always keeps a couple bottles of *shochu* in his room." Mas smiled. Gandhi was an Issei bachelor—skinny, short, and dark, he was the spitting image of Mohandas Gandhi. "I'll go and ask him for a bottle of that stuff," Mas confidently asserted.

Since we were fed a lot of potatoes in camp, the mess hall workers saved the peelings for brewing *shochu*, a potent Japanese whiskey reminiscent of vodka. The commercially produced version, made from barley, wheat, or rice, has a low alcohol content, but the home brewed concoction packs a wallop. I can't vouch for the validity of the stories, but I recall hearing about a couple of drinkers who had lost their eyesight after partaking.

"It will cost you five dollars," Gandhi laughed. Mas had less than a dollar's worth of loose change in his pocket, but that did not hinder his pursuit for a bottle of *shochu*. Mas, who was an eloquent as well as persistent talker, pressed on and on until Gandhi finally made an offer. He suggested that Mas sexually self-indulge himself in front of him. Whether he was joking or serious, I don't know; Mas never told me what ensued following the request, but he came back with a bottle just the same.

The *shochu* tasted good, and soon I felt as though I were floating on a cloud. I continued to consume the brew until my reflexes began to signal I was on the verge of throwing up. Mas, who was stronger than I and apparently feeling no effect, kept on drinking until it finally caught up with him.

"Hank, I don't feel so good," he groaned.

Being a couple of drinking novices, we had consumed too much alcohol too fast. By that point, there was nothing to do but live out the consequences. It wasn't long before we both began to huff and moan and puke. It was a real mess, but since all my senses were dampened, the odor was not at all repugnant, and cleaning up the goo felt neither repulsive nor denigrating.

As soon as I finished cleaning the goo, though, I heard a "blurp!" and realized Mas had lost control of his bowels. I removed his shirt and used it to take care of the new mess. I could see that he was in pain.

"This is what hell must be like. This must be hell!" he kept repeating.

"Yeah," I agreed. "I know this is hell, because only in hell would I be wiping somebody's ass!"

I weaved my way to the latrine to wash his shirt. It was late afternoon and the snow on the rooftops was beginning to melt and drip. The pathway was turning to slush. The image of the awe-inspiring winter landscape of Manzanar, a heavenly paradise then transformed into puking hell, is permanently embedded in my memory, often remembered with a chuckle and a grin.

* * *

Although Manzanar was a wonderland for some, it was also a living hell for those not accustomed to severe weather. The climate in camp was one of extremes; it was normal for temperatures to range from twenty degrees up to the century mark over the course of a year.

One hot summer day, my friend Kenji and I went to the firebreak near Block 3 and took turns hitting a hardball across the empty sandlot. In the scorching summer heat, we were totally exhausted after less than an hour, then deciding to lie motionless, flat on our backs, letting our hearts thump and our sweat drip down onto the scorching sand. As we lay baking in the sun, all we could see was the cloudless blue sky and, in our peripheral vision, pieces of the High Sierra, the Inyo Mountains, and the Alabama Hills.

"Let's find something easier to do—like climbing a mountain," Kenji suggested.

There was Mount Whitney, but that would require more than a day and we would easily be noticed by the forest rangers.

There was also Mount Williamson, but most likely we would be detected there, too. There's no way to climb the barren Inyo Mountains without being observed, but the Alabama Hills… we'd have no difficulty sneaking out of camp and climbing the northern slope in secret.

By then, it had been more than a year since the camp was founded, and security practice had become rather lenient. There were no armed military police patrolling the grounds in jeeps, and the eight guard towers, which were originally equipped with searchlights, machine guns, and soldiers, were now vacant. Under wartime gas rationing, only an occasional vehicle passed on Highway 395, which paralleled Manzanar, and if we ducked behind the sagebrush we wouldn't be detected.

"How about climbing the Alabama Hills?" I suggested. "They made that movie we saw, *Gunga Din,* in those hills."

"Yeah, and they made all kinds of cowboy movies there. You know, like those John Wayne movies."

"Lone Ranger and Roy Rogers, too."

During the Civil War, some Confederate sympathizers had discovered gold in those hills and named the location Alabama Mine after a famous Confederate battleship. The name eventually morphed into Alabama Hills.

"Hey, maybe we could see them making some movies!" I blurted out with excitement.

"Yeah, let's climb it next Saturday and see what's on the other side! We could hunt for jackrabbits on the way."

"Hunt with a bow and arrow?"

"Nah, we don't have the right kind of wood and we'd need arrowheads and feathers. A slingshot will do. I'll make couple of 'em."

By early Saturday morning, he had two slingshots ready and a couple of *bento* boxes for lunch, from a family friend who was a chef in his block's mess hall. Now we were on our way for a day of hiking over the hill to see some movies in the making.

After making absolutely sure no one was watching us, we crossed the barbed wire fence and strode into the sagebrush terrain. In a short while we saw a structure at a distance on our right. Constructed with adobe and a corrugated tin roof, it had been used by local apple farmers and cattlemen in the late nineteenth and early twentieth centuries. We tried to keep a low profile, fearing the building might be occupied.

It wasn't long before we came to George's Creek. Trying to find a shallow spot to cross, I was amazed at the school of rainbows or browns or whatever they were I could see swimming in the stream. Instead of slingshots we should have brought a string, a hook, and some earthworms.

We finally found a shallow enough crossing, the water coming crotch high and with pan-size trout swarming around us so close we could almost grab them with our bare hands. On the other side, we emptied our shoes of water and we continued on our journey, refreshed and cool.

From Manzanar, the Alabama Hills appeared to be smooth, like gigantic anthills, but as we approached the place we wanted to climb, it became apparent that the route was far steeper, rugged, and intimidating than we had imagined. Having chosen a ravine as our cover, the trek was extremely difficult because of the abundance of loose rocks, ranging in size from pebbles to boulders. Occasionally, we'd go through patches where we'd slide down two feet with each foot of ascent. We didn't dare take the crest line, though; it would have been much easier to travel, since it was smoothed from years of erosion, but it was also in clear sight of travelers on Highway 395. As we approached the last one-hundred-foot stretch to the ridge, it was an almost vertical climb, and I was exhausted from heat and exertion and felt both ready and willing to give up, but Kenji wouldn't let me throw in the towel.

"Just take one step at a time, Hank. You can make it!"

Kenji kept repeating those words as he took my hand and pulled me up the slippery slope. Finally we were at the top. We got on our hands and knees and peered over the ridge, and there appeared the workings of a gold mine. There was nobody in sight, but we nevertheless remained cautious and decided to suppress our urge to investigate, since the prevailing feeling in some circles during that era was "the only good Jap is a dead Jap."

From our vantage point, the granite landscape of those Roy Rogers Westerns was nowhere in sight, and our naive hope of seeing some movie stars was shattered. As we sat on a large jagged rock and devoured our *bento*, gazing down on Manzanar with its checkerboard of tarpapered barracks, we knew there would be peace someday and we wouldn't have to sneak around to enjoy what Mother Nature had created for us to enjoy. We would be able to see the other side of the Alabama Hills, with the rounded granite protrusions randomly covering the sandy valley floor against a backdrop of the beautiful snowcapped Sierra, the birds in the sky and the jackrabbits racing through the sagebrush.

I drove to the Alabama Hills forty years later. I sat atop a granite boulder, and while I watched the clouds sweeping over the valley, I couldn't help but wonder if Kenji, who had suffered an acute heart attack and passed on at the early age of fifty, had ever come back to see the other side of the hill. If he hadn't, perhaps he was right there beside me in spirit then, soaking in the beauty and grandeur of what was once denied us on that hot summer day in 1944.

* * *

Back on the trail to Mount Baldy, pursuing the boot marks in the snow that the previous hikers had left behind, I noticed that the prints were beginning to turn to ice in the shaded area along the trail. Then I witnessed one of the unpredictable, sudden changes in temperature that so often occur at high altitudes: the snow suddenly turned to rain. As I gained altitude, the wind began to blow, which then chilled the air to sub-zero temperatures. I was without a doubt inadequately dressed. My pants were soon soaking wet, and although my water-resistant parka was just what it claimed to be, it was no protection against the cold. As the raindrops turned to hail, I began to wonder which of the three I would prefer: snow, rain, or hail. Not that I had any choice.

The three hikers who had passed me earlier were on their trek down.

"How was it up there?" I asked.

"Hey, it's great up there. You're almost there!" One hiker flashed me an encouraging grin.

Icicles were hanging from my cap's visor, and I could see a chunk of ice clinging to the lower rim of my trifocals. The wind was beginning to pick up, and visibility was down to about two hundred yards. I was the only hiker on the uphill trail, and I became terrified and afraid. I turned around to start the trip back to my vehicle. But a few minutes later, I made another about-face and continued on the uphill climb; I had seen a hiker coming up the trail on a switchback in the distance. I now had company.

"I'll let you pass. I'm a slow hiker," I said as I stepped aside for a man with a goatee.

"There are six of us," he said, and he pointed to his companions, about fifty yards behind him.

"We're turning back," one of the hikers shouted.

"Going back to the car?" the hiker with the goatee yelled back.

"We'll wait for you at the ski hut," someone answered.

As we were already almost at the summit, it wasn't long before the hiker who'd passed me had reached the top of Mount Baldy and was on his way down.

"How was it up there?" I asked, which in retrospect was a

silly question, because what else could it be but gusty and freezing cold?

"It was so cold I just stayed there a minute," he said.

His gray goatee was now white, covered with sparkling ice crystals. His visor was a mere chunk of ice, and his navy blue parka was spotted with glistening ice patches. The wind was blowing at more than forty-five miles an hour and the ice crystals in the air began to dance and swirl in waves as they fell onto the snowy ground, almost instantly covering our footprints. It was the first time I had experienced such a sight, and I stopped for a moment and stood in awe. Visibility was now down to less than fifty yards.

Even ten seconds at the summit was more than I could bear. The thermometer dangling from my backpack strap was covered with ice and unreadable. I cracked the ice open and read the windchill at twenty-two degrees below zero Fahrenheit. I guessed I was the last hiker on the trail and, with the visibility diminishing and my footsteps disappearing as I made them, I knew I had to hurry fast to a lower elevation. My trifocals were just a chunk of ice, and fearing damage to the glasses if I placed them in the backpack, I just lowered them down over my nose. The rims obstructed my view, and I was further hindered by the thin layer of ice that coated my eyelashes. Each step down was a hit-or-miss affair: if I hit the snow-covered ground, it was fine, but when I stepped on top of a snow-camouflaged manzanita bush, it was like walking into a sinkhole; I'd suddenly drop down and be up to my waist in snow before hitting solid ground. I did my best to hurry along and keep the goatee hiker in sight so he could lead me down the snow-covered trail.

Why do people want to go through all this? Why do we punish ourselves by exposing ourselves to rain, ice, snow, and extreme temperatures? I asked myself. Why not be cuddled up in the comfort of a nice warm den at home watching television? Perhaps the driving force was my zealous aspiration of climbing to the top of Mount Whitney. Perhaps this was my way of trying to prepare myself by being exposed to every conceivable weather condition I might have to confront on the trail to the Big One. I'd wondered before why teachers went to Manzanar to teach, when they could have secured jobs in more comfortable environments during the war.

* * *

This was during an era when sashimi was not considered a food that a civilized person would consume. An era when "Japs" were depicted in cartoons with slanted eyes, yellow faces, and protruding buck teeth chomping on raw fish and rice balls. Ugh! So why did white folks choose to teach at Manzanar and risk being called "Jap lovers"? Also, weather-wise, there are many places more appealing and comfortable than Manzanar, with its dust storms in the summer and snowstorms in the winter.

Mr. Rogers, a French language teacher who was in his mid-twenties, was a Navy veteran, and his left shoulder was deformed from a military injury. He spoke twenty of the sixty major languages of the world and was knowledgeable in and fascinated by the various customs and languages of this planet. He of course spoke Japanese and was interested in Japanese culture. This was probably his reason for choosing to teach at Manzanar.

My friend Mas and I were students in Mr. Rogers's class. At the time, Mas was infatuated with a girl who lived in his block and wanted to woo her with a bottle of Chanel No. 5. It cost five dollars and was unavailable at the camp store, so he asked Mr. Rogers to pick it up for him on his upcoming trip to Los Angeles. Mr. Rogers graciously agreed to honor Mas's request, and when he returned from Los Angeles with the bottle, Mas and I visited him at his apartment. We walked to the southeastern corner of camp and registered with the sentry guarding what was known as the "Caucasian residential area." The sentry studied his clipboard, where Mr. Rogers had left our names, and then directed us to Apartment 25. The buildings were shorter in length than our barracks, and the walls were lined with wood, painted white, and had gardens in front, giving them the appearance of a group of homey little cottages.

Mr. Rogers welcomed us into his apartment and served us pie and Coke. After handing over the Chanel No. 5 to Mas, Mr. Rogers invited us to sit down and look at some of the photos he had taken at Manzanar.

"Where you gonna go when the war's over?" I asked.

"Well," he paused for a moment, "I'd like to go to Japan, since I've never been there. From the pictures I've seen and from what I've heard, it's definitely a fascinating country."

"So you gonna teach English out there?" Mas asked.

"I don't know. There might be other lucrative opportunities there."

Meanwhile, in the Pacific theater, the U.S. Marines were drawing out the members of the Imperial Army from their pillboxes in Okinawa. The curtain was beginning to fall upon a war that had brought havoc and sorrow to millions of people, both the Allies and Axis. On the home front, people from Manzanar were relocating to various parts of the country. It was the last semester for Manzanar High School, and we waved farewell to friends and neighbors on a daily basis. Mas's first love had relocated to Idaho but they kept exchanging love notes until one day he received a Dear John letter. Apparently, the girl's sisters and mother did not approve of their correspondence. Teachers, too, left Manzanar at semester's end for various parts of the world and, like missionaries, they chose their destinations based on where they were needed most—some to nearby cities and some afar, like Mr. Rogers.

It was eight years later, when I was stationed in Tokyo with the U.S. Army, that I phoned the various military departments and units to see if Mr. Rogers was there; if he had gone to

Japan, Tokyo would certainly be the most likely city for him. After several days of calling various military and civilian agencies, I located him and we arranged to meet at his hotel. They say that a teacher remembers only the best students and the worst students and, being in the latter category, I was apparently memorable. Mr. Rogers treated me to a lunch, over which we had a long chat and looked at the photo album from his Manzanar days. It was an emotional reunion to say the least, especially in a land many thousand miles away from where we had originally met.

I visit Manzanar often, and I always pay tribute to the teachers who once lived in those white cottages by Bairs Creek. The concrete doorsteps are now all that remain of their homes in the desert. The teachers are rarely mentioned in the story of Manzanar. Sometimes they are completely ignored and forgotten. But I remember.

I also often remember and cherish the camaraderie that developed in Manzanar. When that last school term was over and summer vacation arrived, I joined my friends to work on a roofing crew. There was Ben, Roy, Wanger, Raymond, and me, all sixteen-year-olds entering the workforce for the first time, for sixteen dollars a month.

We had the cook at Block 27 make us an early breakfast and then we walked to the warehouses, at the southern edge of camp. We arrived at the carpentry warehouse, where hundreds of rolls of tarpaper were stored and began with loading twenty rolls onto an olive drab army truck.

"I'll drive the truck to Block 16, and you can drive it back after we get through," Roy said to me.

Block 16 was an elementary school and therefore empty during summer vacation. It was sunrise by the time we started rolling out the paper on the roof and then pouring tar along the seams. By eight o'clock, we were already feeling the heat radiating from the roof, and by nine o'clock, the tarpaper was softening. We had to be extremely careful when hammering the nails because if we pounded too hard, the nail would rip through the soft tarpaper and into the wood below, leaving a hole in the roofing material. As it approached ten o'clock, we began to rush back and forth across the roof, unrolling, pouring tar, and hammering the nails as fast as we could to beat the heat. We were racing against Mother Nature's blistering temperature, which we knew was going to surpass the century mark that day. By the time we got to the last fifty-foot strip, across the roof ridge, we had to slow down and lay it softly, hammering the tacks carefully and tenderly since the tarpaper was by then hot and limp, and any careless pulling or tugging would rip it to pieces.

"The tar's beginning to run," Roy yelled. The gooey tar had melted to a thin liquid, and it was time to call it a day. We descended and stood on the sand, staring at the countless black tar marks streaking across the roof.

"What a shitty job," Ben remarked. We stood in silence, for no one could argue.

That evening after chow, I heard someone shout, "Fire! Look at that black smoke!"

I joined a group from our block and walked toward the southern edge of camp. "Maybe it's the motor pool. Looks like oil burning," someone guessed.

By the time we arrived, the outer tarpaper coverings and walls constructed of one-by-twelve wooden planks had already burned off, and the skeleton frame of two-by-fours was glowing red hot, emitting flames high into the atmosphere. It was the carpentry warehouse where we had picked up the tarpaper that morning. The combination of paint, lacquer, tarpaper, and other flammable substances quickly turned it into a pile of charcoal and ashes.

Mr. Samejima, our foreman, was there. "It's going to be a

while before we get another shipment of tarpaper, so tomorrow you guys should come here and clean this up. Maybe we can find some nails and cabinet hardware that we can salvage."

The following morning, we scrounged around for usable hardware. Beneath the ashes, we found boxes of hinges, nails, screws, and other hardware. All were black, some were melted, others were warped, and only a few were salvageable. With other wartime priorities taking precedence, carpentry work for the camp would have to be postponed indefinitely.

The clean-up completed, I passed by Block 16 and took a final look at the last barrack we had roofed. The ugly dripping streaks of tar now appeared as gentle teardrops in the late hazy afternoon sun against picturesque Mount Williamson. It seemed a farewell to our young roofing crew and was a small comfort to the despair of losing the warehouse and the job, not to mention our brotherly camaraderie. The Block 16 elementary school was never reopened, and the barracks we reroofed were never used. They were torn down the following year for scrap lumber.

* * *

Since I was the last hiker descending the mountain and those footprints in the snow were being covered within moments, I could not risk losing sight of the goateed hiker. As I descended and the snow eased up, the trail finally became visible again, and I was confident I could make it back to the bottom on my own. Feeling cold and sick, and suspecting that these were early signs of hypothermia, I continued my descent at a slower pace. By the time I reached the truck, my hands were so numb and my whole body was shivering so violently that I couldn't even fish the keys out of my pocket.

Trembling, I trudged up to a young sightseer who had just stepped out of his car and asked, "Could you get my keys out of my back pocket?" I turned my butt toward him. He gave me a sheepish smile and walked away. Fortunately, his friend, seeing my wet clothing and appraising my dilemma, reluctantly helped me with the keys.

Now I desperately needed to go to the bathroom, but it was absolutely impossible to open my fly with my numb fingers, and I wouldn't dare ask a stranger to do it for me; if they thought I was a pervert for asking for help with my keys, they wouldn't take well to a request to open up my fly.

Well, why bother unzipping the fly? I told myself. *I'm already soaking wet from head to toe!*

I had come down from the mountain feeling invincible, but that triumph was now completely extinguished, since peeing in one's pants is not consistent with the image of an indestructible man.

Chapter Seven

TWENTY-FIVE-DOLLAR STIPEND

The sky was clear and the weather was calm but just a bit nippy as I parked the truck and began to prepare for the hike.

I had a jacket over my T-shirt, and one pint of water seemed sufficient, since I could always take in a mouthful of snow, as I often had in the past.

My hiking friend Wilson had just arrived at the parking area.

"There's fresh snow on the trail. You think there's a lot up there at the top?" I asked.

"It seems like there will be. It was a day like this several winters ago that I got lost."

"Right here on Mount Baldy?" I was surprised and even skeptical of Wilson's story, since he had been mountaineering since the late forties. That's a half century of experience.

"I started to walk down the mountain in the wrong direction, and my dog kept barking and wouldn't follow me. You know, he led me to safety. He passed away a few years ago, but he saved my life that day."

Saved his life? I couldn't imagine an experienced hiker being so disoriented on Baldy that his life was threatened.

He opened the trunk of his car and took out his backpack.

"You could go on ahead. I'll catch up with you later," he said. He always spent five to ten minutes checking his gear and supply of snacks and food before leaving on his treks.

Halfway up the mountain was a ski hut built in the late 1920s by the Sierra Club. As I approached, I saw it was occupied by a Boy Scout troop, mostly fifteen to seventeen years of age.

"You guys camped out here last night?" I asked one of the parents.

"We came up last night when it began to snow and had a hard time finding this place in the dark. We almost gave up and were ready to camp out in the open about a hundred yards from here."

"Bet it was cold last night with all this snow."

"Yeah, we were lucky we found this hut."

I sat on an exposed boulder nearby for a snack and a drink, and to decide whether to attempt the hike to the summit. The trail was covered with two feet of snow, and my only other option to get to the top was to scale the face of Mount Baldy.

A scoutmaster came out of the hut, scraped the seemingly fresh snow off the top of a snowbank with his hand, and scooped it into a pan to boil for a hot drink.

"Hey, that's the way to do it," one of the scouts remarked to his peer.

I kept a straight face and kept chewing on my trail mix as I vividly recalled a hiker making a piss stop the previous week at the very spot about to become the next cup of coffee.

I sat on the boulder debating whether to plow through the snow on the trail or call it quits and return to the truck. When Wilson came up the trail with his aluminum cane, making the ever familiar click-clack noise, I decided that I'd just do what Wilson did.

"The trail is covered with two feet of snow," I told him.

Wilson studied the trail, looked toward the summit of Mount Baldy, and then motioned with his head for me to follow him up to the summit. *He's crazy*, I thought, since I'd never seen anyone climb straight up the face of the mountain. I didn't know whether he was serious or just joking, so I stood and watched him for a moment. When I realized he was serious, I decided to follow him. What the heck.

The face of the mountain was covered with a foot of packed snow, which helped us get at least a semi-firm footing. But in making a near-vertical climb in the thin air of almost ten thousand feet above sea level, I was totally exhausted by the time I reached the midpoint. Resting every twenty-five steps thereafter, I finally reached the crest. I looked for Wilson, but he was already on the Devil's Backbone trail, a less treacherous route that led back to the parking area. The six feet of snow at the summit had turned to a solid mass of ice, covering any landmarks that might have existed. It began to get breezy and cold then, and out of nowhere, clouds began to sweep in. The subzero wind was carrying a dense fog across the top of the mountain; visibility was no more than fifty feet.

Just like that, I was caught in a whiteout. With no landmarks and almost no visibility, it was like being in a dark room. I had no sense of direction at all. Panicked and scared, I hastily made an unwise decision to hike down the slope in the direction I thought Wilson had gone. With no visible footprints on the ice, however, I could only make a random guess. My crampon spikes made it extremely difficult for me to descend straight down the steep slope of ice, and as a result, I began to travel down at an angle, which in retrospect was a grave mistake. I ended up going around the top of the mountain to the other side and then down into another valley. As I made it below the cloud cover and visibility got better, I realized my surroundings were totally unfamiliar. I was lost. Again.

* * *

In 1943, internees seventeen years and older had to make a decision that would determine their future, and it all came down to a couple of straightforward "yes" or "no" answers. Some decisions were well thought out, some were emotional, but many were made by people lost as to what to do, and their decisions were random and hasty, with calamitous outcomes.

The government asked, briefly stated, if internees were willing to serve in the United Stated Armed Forces and whether or not we were willing to break all ties with Japan. These are commonly referred to as questions 27 and 28 on the so-called loyalty questionnaire.

When I was on my way to the latrine one afternoon, I noticed a group of older Nisei in front of a barrack doorstep engaged in what appeared to a heated discussion. I quietly snuck behind them to listen in on the conversation. Two men were sitting on the steps and five others were gathered around them.

"If you answer 'no' and 'no,' you'll be sent to Japan after the war," one man remarked.

"What's wrong with that? At least we won't be treated like pieces of shit," another argued.

"Yeah. Besides, *you* won't be drafted into the army," another man laughed. Each one seemed to have an opinion.

"What's wrong with being drafted? Your brother is a tech sergeant serving in the army and he has it made."

"Well, according to his last letter, he's on one of those small Pacific islands where it's hot and humid and miserable, and he said it's a living hell."

"I'm going with 'yes, yes,'" butted in one of the men sitting on the steps.

"You're an asshole. I'll go with 'no' on twenty-seven but 'yes' on twenty-eight, because I never had ties with Japan to begin with," his friend added.

Everyone in camp was talking about questions 27 and 28. Reactions were mixed and emotions were high. Many were undecided and weighing each other's opinions about what to do.

"Ben is going to answer 'no, no,'" Mother informed Edith and me that evening. He had been hanging around with Saka-guchi, a troublemaker, and Mother was convinced that he had influenced Ben because Sakaguchi, a Kibei, had returned to this country only a few months before his eighteenth birthday to evade being drafted into the Japanese army. Mother felt that his heart and loyalty still remained in Japan.

"What are you going to do?" I asked mother.

"I don't know" was her immediate reply. She decided to consult Mr. Muro, the leader of the camp's Seicho-no-Ie church meetings.

"Answer 'yes,'" Mr. Muro advised without a moment's hesitation. "America is still the best place to live in the whole world."

"With Ben gone, who's going to take care of the farm that we left behind, once we're allowed to go back? Edith will be married, and Shozo is only a child." Mother felt helpless.

After considering our predicament, he said, "You could sell the farm," which came as a surprise. "You can come to Los Angeles when the war is over and live in my hotel. Everything's going to turn out all right. I promise!" Mr. Muro owned a lease on a hotel in downtown Los Angeles, and his Mexican American wife continued to operate it during his absence. For Mother, Mr. Muro's words were as good as gold.

The following winter, a bus stopped between the mess hall entrance and our barrack. Since the ground was covered with patches of snow, I stood inside the warm house, by the window in my room, and watched Ben's family and some other friends waiting with their luggage to board the bus. They would ride to Mojave and transfer to a train to Tule Lake Relocation Center, which had been turned into a segregation center for those who answered "no, no" and were therefore deemed disloyal by the government.

My brother Sam and his wife, Kiyoko, had been at Topaz Relocation Center and also answered "no, no," joining Ben's family at Tule Lake with their newborn son, Glen. So did Yosh and my sister Miharu, who made the trip to Tule Lake from Amache Relocation Center with their infant son, Dan. Those three households were again reunited.

Later, Yosh and Miharu took the option of rescinding their "no, no" positions and moved to Seabrook Farms in New Jersey, joining 2,500 other evacuees working on the farm. Shortly after the war ended, Yosh's family returned to Central California.

At Tule Lake, Ben and Sam joined the pro-Japan militant group. Every morning at the crack of dawn, with bandanas around their foreheads, they jogged around the Tule Lake camp chanting, "*Wah'shoi, wah'shoi*," earning the group the moniker Wah'shoi Boys. (*Wah'shoi* was just a meaningless chant to keep them in step.) While some saw them as gallant and fearless, the U.S. military didn't take kindly to the demeanor of the Wah'shoi Boys, and both Ben and Sam, among others, were sent to Fort Lincoln Internment Camp in Bismarck, North Dakota. German Americans and German immigrants were also confined there, and after the war Sam often told us stories about the Nisei team playing baseball against the Germans.

When the war ended, Ben and Sam had the option to rescind their "no, no" positions and return to the West Coast and reunite with their families, but there was a slight glitch. Both Ben and Sam tried to discuss and coordinate their plans for the future with their wives at Tule Lake, but while their correspondence slowly passed back and forth across half the continent by mail, and confusion and red tape caused further delay, the deadline to rescind their "no, no" position expired. Although they *were* united with their families, they were also placed on a slow boat to Japan.

Living in Japan was not easy for Nisei who left the States after the war. They were coldly received in the devastated country, which was experiencing a shortage of food and other basic commodities. Sam often described the predicament by telling the story of how they had to use straw as a substitute for toilet paper upon debarking at Kobe.

While interned at Fort Lincoln, Ben had enrolled in a home study course in air conditioning and refrigeration, and being an eloquent talker, he quickly procured a position as an air conditioning technician with a United States occupation force based in Osaka. He spent the remaining days of his eighty-two years in Osaka, while Sam and Kiyoko, with their sons Glen and Aki, returned to California in 1959 to start their life anew.

* * *

I was totally lost on the opposite side of the mountain. My several similar experiences had taught me that the best option was to take a piss, stop, relax, think, and just go back to where I'd come from.

"Baldy is the tallest peak around here, so all I have to do is continue walking up and up and up," I repeated to myself as I trudged my way to the top, with visibility again at almost nil. I waited at the summit until the all-encompassing cloud had dissipated.

With snow and ice, wind, and freezing temperatures, with zero visibility and no identifiable landmarks, I realized I was in a life-and-death situation. If this had happened a year earlier, when I was less experienced, I probably would have continued to descend the slope, which leads to Fish Fork and San Gabriel River many miles west. I would have had neither the endurance nor the time to make it out of the snow-covered canyon and could have frozen to death.

As one forest ranger jokingly remarked when I came down a mountain trail one day under similar circumstances, shivering in my T-shirt, "We sure would have hated to fish a chunk of frozen meat out of there." Often our choice comes down to being fresh meat or frozen.

Even though I'd waited out the whiteout, I was still disoriented and figured my best option was to follow a set of footprints—which I thought were mine—down the mountain. With snow canvassing the terrain, the protruding pine trees all looked the same. Although unable to recognize any landmarks, I continued the trek down, occasionally sensing that I was on the wrong trail but hoping it would intersect with a trail that would lead me back to the right place. I kept following the footprints, and as I came to a steep slope, fear began to creep in. I felt afraid that if I slipped and fell into the ravine, I might never be able to climb back up. I came to the final realization that this was indeed the wrong trail.

"I might as well keep following the footprints. Going down is at least easier than climbing back up in that snow," I reasoned.

As I approached the eastern ridge of West Baldy, I was relieved to see four members of the Sheriff's Search and Rescue Team scanning the valley below them.

"Have you seen a lost hiker?" one of the team members asked.

"No," I said. "Somebody got lost?"

"Yeah, we're looking for a guy with a yellow jacket and Levi's."

I looked at myself, since I was lost, too. I was wearing jeans, but instead of a yellow jacket, I had a green one.

I asked the fellow where they had come from.

"We came from the village on this Baldy Trail," he answered.

Now that I knew I was on Baldy Trail, all I had to do was follow it to my truck. I took a long confident stride, making each step with conviction to project the appearance that I was a hardy, experienced hiker, instead of the hardly experienced, lost hiker I was.

* * *

I was sixteen in Manzanar, adrift and confused, like a lost hiker in a whiteout. It was an age of mixed emotions as I transitioned from childhood to adulthood. It was 1945, and the tide had turned. The high-altitude B-19s and the low-flying B-24s on bombing missions were dropping incendiary bombs as well as leaflets over Tokyo, printed in Japanese and telling the people to surrender. We knew then that the war would soon be over. The ban on Japanese people living on the West Coast was lifted in February of 1945, and internees were returning to their homes. From camp, we were waving farewell to our friends and neighbors.

To help the resettlement process and to ease the transition, the government allowed adults eighteen years of age and older to leave Manzanar for a month so they could make arrangements for work and housing before returning to camp to prepare for permanent relocation. My friend Raymond was planning to join his father in Linden, near Sacramento, where they had owned a peach orchard prior to the evacuation. His father had spent the previous month repossessing the farm, and some friends and I decided to invite ourselves over, hoping we might get a job on the farm.

Raymond, Roy, Ben, Wanger, and I applied for short-term-leave permits from camp but were at first refused because of our age. We were sixteen but needed to be eighteen. We presented a lame argument that our aging parents could not speak English and were depending on us to prepare for the relocation, and although the man at the office surely didn't believe us, he nevertheless agreed to grant the release if it was approved by our parents. After receiving written permission from our parents, we were off to Linden, finally free after three years of confinement.

On that early June morning, there were other Manzanites leaving on buses for their respective locales. The first stop was the Mojave train depot, where we got off and loitered around the station. The bus continued on to Los Angeles, but we were waiting for the train. When we heard the train approaching the station, Wanger started crooning, "Do you hear that whistle down the line? I figure that it's engine number forty-nine." We looked at each other, taking him for a loony. He continued, "She's the only one that'll sound that way, on the Atchison, Topeka, and the Santa Fe."

Suddenly, there was a train in front of us with Atchison, Topeka, and Santa Fe printed on its side. Wanger was singing one of the top hit tunes of 1945, and there was nobody more surprised than he himself to actually see an Atchison, Topeka, and Santa Fe train in front of his very eyes.

When we boarded the train, we were in for a shock. Only Pullman cars were available, and although they were occupied by only a handful of passengers, it was inconceivable then for "Japs" to ride with respectable people in the first-class sleeper cars. Instead, we were placed in the men's restroom lounge. We didn't mind it, actually. We talked and joked all the way to Stockton, having a good time, humming and singing the Atchison, Topeka song. The only offensive thing about it at the time was the odor.

Joe met us at Stockton railway depot. Joe was of German descent and a longtime friend and neighbor of Roy's family. He owned land adjoining Roy's farm, and while Roy's family was at Manzanar, Joe had looked after their fifteen-acre tomato ranch. Joe drove us in his red Ford pickup truck to Raymond's family's farm in Linden. When we met Raymond's father, we did not receive the welcome that we'd hoped for. Raymond was severely reprimanded for bringing us there, since the harvesting season was over and there were no jobs. Raymond had to remain with his father while the rest of us returned to Joe's.

From Joe's farm, we strode over to Roy's home, since it was within walking distance and Roy was rapt with nostalgia over seeing the house he'd grown up in.

Inside the house we found five Filipino men slouched around a table eating. (Roy's family had rented their house to Filipino workers while they were at Manzanar.) The men stared at us without speaking, and an incredible fear overcame all of us, since we'd heard of the atrocities that the Imperial Japanese soldiers had inflicted upon their families in the Philippines during the Japanese conquest. We figured these men wouldn't take an easy liking to us. I inched backward to the exit, and as soon as I was out the door, I hurried toward Joe's house, never looking back.

Joe's one-room wooden house was attached to the barn where he kept his farm equipment. It was also used as a bunkhouse to accommodate hired hands during the harvesting season. There was no electricity, so we struck a few matches and shuffled around on the dirt floor in the semidarkness until we found two steel bunks. They didn't have mattresses, and it appeared as though the building hadn't been used for a few years due to lack of help during the war years. Exhausted from our trip, we jumped in bed, doubling up, and were soon away in dreamland.

With sunrise came another surprise. Everything around us—the horse harnesses hanging on the wall, the farm implements lying on the ground—was covered with spiderwebs, which, upon further examination, we saw belonged to shiny black creatures with red hourglass logos on their bellies. We got out of there pretty quick.

That day, Joe had to go into town, so we tagged along and looked in the newspapers and asked around for jobs, but to no avail. Joe also asked his friends and neighbors and passed the word along, but since harvesting season was over, there were no jobs in sight.

We were all broke, and all we could do was wait and hope for a miracle. We had nothing to eat. One day passed, two days passed, and three days passed without food or drink. We were too proud to ask Joe for food; besides, he most likely did not have enough to feed all of us for so long. Probably the worst part was not having water during that time. Joe's hand-pumped well was located only a yard or so from his outhouse, and even though Joe drank from it, we figured he was probably immune but that we'd become ill if we tried. By the fourth day, we were hungry, thirsty, and desperate. We collected sixty-eight cents among the four of us and walked to the closest market and bought a bottle of mustard, a loaf of bread, and two large bottles of Royal Crown Cola. On our return trip, we picked some apricots growing in the cemetery lot and took some discarded onions from a recently harvested field. After slicing the rotten portions off the onions, we made onion and mustard sandwiches that tasted better than anything we had ever eaten.

Finally, Joe brought us the news that nearby Mandeville Island was hiring. As he left, he sheepishly warned us: "That's the last place you would want to go."

The next morning, Joe drove us to the Port of Stockton, where we boarded a twenty-two-foot motorboat. Mandeville was a privately owned eight-thousand-acre island in the Sacramento Delta where they grew potatoes, carrots, tomatoes, and other crops. There were many harvesting camps on the island, each one self-sufficient, with living quarters, showers, outhouses, and a kitchen for the workers. We were at Camp 21 and slept on the second floor of a barn that had space for about twenty bunks. It was comfortable, all things considered, although during the late evening and into the morning hours we began to shiver without blankets. One night I dragged an unused mattress from the storage shed and sandwiched myself between it and the mattresses I was lying on, making my sleeping arrangements warm and comfortable for the remainder of our stay.

I was put on a celery planting machine. Luckily it didn't last long, though; the area was reclaimed swampland, the soil consisted of small to microscopic decayed reed particles resembling garden peat moss, and my sensitive skin immediately broke into an unbearable rash. Fortunately, the celery planting was over in a week and I was assigned to a swamping job in a shed, toting hundred-pound potato sacks and dumping their contents into a bin, from which women workers would take the potatoes and slice them into four to six pieces for planting, which was what Roy, Ben, and Wanger had to do in the hot sun.

Although the evenings were cold, temperatures were over one hundred degrees during the day. It was so hot, one evening we saw a huge fire that had sparked when hundreds of hay bales, stacked two stories high, became so heated during the day that they just burst into a blaze by themselves. It was spontaneous combustion, an unforgettable, spectacular sight, a gigantic bonfire in the middle of nowhere. It was far off enough in the distance that no souls or structures were in danger. We stood and watched, stupefied, until the pulsating blue flares began to fade into a restrained amber flame.

Since I was the only male at the potato shed, I was often asked to run an errand in the truck. To conserve gas, the muffler on the truck had been removed, and without it the two-ton truck sounded like a Harley-Davidson. Tearing down the dry dirt road created a burst of dust which looked like a thunderhead. All my tensions and frustrations seemed to evaporate with the dust as it dissipated in the air.

After several weeks working for sixty-five cents an hour, for ten hours a day, it was time to leave the island. We boarded the Southern Pacific train and proceeded to Bakersfield. Being extremely tired, I slumped in the seat, spread my legs, and soon was on cloud nine when *wham!* Someone had kicked my foot. Thinking at first it was just a nightmare, I opened my eyes and saw a porter staring down at me and saying, "Get your foot out of the aisle!" As he continued down the aisle, I heard him mumbling something I was unable to understand, but I knew that it wasn't anything complimentary.

At Bakersfield, we transferred to a bus that took us into Los Angeles. Since Wanger and Ben were from L.A., they were going to show Roy and me, a couple of country hicks, what a real city looked like. Mr. Muro invited us to stay at the skid row hotel his wife was operating. At the bus depot, we asked the taxi driver to drive us to Mrs. Muro's address, to which the driver sneered and said, "It's only a few blocks. Why don't you walk?" and then he continued to chat with his fellow drivers, completely ignoring us. So we walked—lost and in circles for blocks and blocks, lugging our heavy luggage and making nasty remarks at Wanger, since he was supposed to know the way around town.

Finally we arrived at the hotel and unpacked our bags. Then we walked to Broadway. I was stunned at the sight of all the magnificent movie theaters, beautiful department stores, and spotlessly clean sidewalks. I was gaping at the tall buildings when I bumped into a Marine decorated with rows of ribbons. It was obvious he had just returned from combat.

"*Konnichiwa,*" (hello) the Marine said.

What a friendly Marine, I thought, as I smiled and said, "*Konnichiwa.*"

He looked at his buddy and said, "Yeah, he's a Jap," and they both continued down Broadway. I was angry, but there was nothing I could do besides just stand on the sidewalk, stupefied and humiliated.

That night at the hotel was a complete disaster. After midnight, my arms started itching, followed by my belly and my legs.

Everyone began to scratch, but we were too exhausted to bother finding out what the culprit was. When Ben finally turned on the lights, there they were! Tiny black bedbugs! We were each bitten in rows, each mark an inch to two inches apart down a straight line, and the itching was much worse than that from mosquitoes. Thank goodness this was the last day of our short-term leave before we had to return to Manzanar.

We departed Los Angeles on a bus the following day and arrived back at Manzanar in time to make the evening chow line. Somehow, I felt different. I had a different outlook toward life, a different attitude, a slightly more mature philosophy. Perhaps I had also matured physically and emotionally. I even became more appreciative of the pork chop, mashed potato, and canned spinach on my plate. I sat in front of Ralph and Leo, both several years my senior, who had recently returned from picking potatoes in Idaho.

"Looks like you just got back," asked Leo as he chopped up his pork chop. So where did you go?"

"Stockton."

"How much is the cathouse there?" Ralph asked.

Without hesitation, I took a quick guess and, with a straight face, said, "Five bucks."

"You know," Ralph grinned and continued, "a guy is not a man until he goes to one of those places. I guess you're a man now, Hank." We all laughed.

Later, as I stepped off the stairs of my barrack, on my way to the shower, that picturesque, serene, and majestic Mount Williamson appeared different to me, too. The snow had melted and it seemed like a gigantic mass of cold, gray granite, protruding from the earth as though it were ready to swallow anything in its path. To the left was the barbed wire fence against the rust-colored Inyo Mountains, desolate, cold, and lonely. *Beyond that fence is the real world*, I thought. *A bitter, harsh, and, without doubt, hostile world.*

As I opened the shower house door, goose pimples appeared on my skin. More than half of the inhabitants of our block had already relocated to various parts of the country, and the once busy shower room was now empty. The noise and laughter were gone, replaced by the spray of a lone showerhead reverberating in the empty room. The lonely and frightening feeling continued to overwhelm me.

The future appeared bleak, unpredictable, and uncertain. Would I be able to overcome the challenges, or would I succumb to the insurmountable obstacles lurking beyond that fence? I came to realize that my warm, friendly, sheltered, and carefree life would soon be over, and Manzanar would be but a memory.

"We're leaving Manzanar with Muro-*san* and going to stay at his hotel," Mother told me two weeks after I'd returned home. We were among the fortunate ones. Manzanar camp was being closed, and people were being ordered to evacuate by November 1945, whether or not they had homes or jobs to return to. The Justice Department did, however, provide each person with twenty-five dollars and a free ticket to any destination in the world.

When people arrived at Manzanar, there was at least food and shelter. Now, they had neither. Starting a life from square one, with a twenty-five dollar stipend, the hardships and challenges had just begun.

Chapter Eight

A LIFE IN SKID ROW

It was one of those lazy, hazy days in June when the sun was refusing to shine through and you would rather stay in bed until noon. I arrived at the Mount Baldy Village at 5:30 a.m., while a four-foot-tall black bear was making its morning rounds, invading the trash cans looking for her breakfast. By midmorning I was perspiring as I tramped up the trail, and with high humidity and no breeze, I wished I had hiked along the beach rather than climb a mountain with a six-thousand-foot elevation gain.

At eight thousand feet, I noticed a black object across the trail. It began to move, and upon closer examination, I saw it was a four-foot-long rattler. I let it slither past me into the brushes as I watched in bewilderment. I had come across ten other rattlers in my life, including one called a Mojave Green that was even longer, at six feet! It had covered the entire width of a jeep trail as it slowly passed. But I had never seen a rattlesnake at an elevation above six thousand feet. This was also the first time I had seen a black rattler.

Farther up the trail, I began to notice a slight cool breeze, which was soothing but not enough to relieve the pain in my feet. By the time I reached the Baldy summit, I was exhausted and sore. I sat on the ground against a huge boulder, joining the other hikers who had come up the Devil's Backbone and Ski Hut trails.

The valley below me was covered with a fluffy blanket of white clouds, and protruding above that layer were several mountain peaks, like islands floating in the sky. All around me, the earth was but a white, velvety mass. I sat hunched against the boulder, absorbing the heavenly landscape, taking in a view seemingly untouched by civilization, as serene and peaceful as it could be. I tilted my cap over my eyes while the stray strands of my shabby snow-white hair danced in the mountain breeze. I was content, for this is what I yearned for in my retirement years. Finally I was sitting on top of the world.

Finally gone was the time when it seemed like every day held an exciting challenge, when I was full of dreams, overflowing with hope and fascination. With every turn in life, I experienced something new; with each moment of despair, I raised my hopes; and with each shattered dream, I came up with another to take its place.

* * *

I was sixteen when I was introduced to life among the unique populace of Los Angeles's skid row. Immediately after relocating from Manzanar to L.A., Mother, Edith, and I made our home in Mr. Muro's hotel in a room that was nine by twelve and furnished with amenities including a cold water washbasin in one corner, a single community toilet at the end of the hall for over half a dozen families, and a bathtub door that was opened upon request.

The floor underneath the toilet was askew, leaning at a three-degree angle, and the water tank was placed high on the wall with a dangling chain we pulled to flush. The stench was permanently absorbed into the floor and walls; removing the reek was an impossible task.

The hotel was built above a café and consisted of eight rooms. The Muro family, our landlords, occupied Rooms 1 and 2, and were in the room across the hall.

Mr. Muro was in his fifties, about five feet tall and wiry, with a dark complexion, a pronounced jaw and sharp cheek features, and a spritely disposition. His enthusiasm was contagious; he always had a positive attitude that made the listeners of his talks about Seicho-no-Ie philosophy feel glad they were alive. The Seicho-no-Ie faith was a based on the concept that God was the almighty force that guided us through our lives. Hardships and misfortunes were not calamities but blessings in disguise, avenues for a happy and prosperous tomorrow. Mother had regularly attended Seicho-no-Ie meetings while we were in camp.

In an era when interracial marriage was frowned upon in the Nikkei (Japanese American) culture in the United States, Mr. Muro had boldly tied the knot with Mrs. Muro, a third-generation Mexican American. Mrs. Muro was slightly taller than her husband and on the hefty side, with a heart just as large. She and Mr. Muro adopted Hope, a Nisei girl born in 1930. They raised her as though she were their own biological daughter.

"This is my wife, and this is Hope, our daughter," Mr. Muro had introduced us when his family had visited Manzanar. At twelve, Hope was two years younger than I. Her face was snowy white, and her jet black hair was cut straight at chin-length and had bangs. In her white blouse and pleated black skirt, she looked like a typical Catholic schoolgirl. She was shy and very well-mannered, and with a slight change in hairdo (getting rid of those bangs), she would have been a very attractive girl.

"Hi," I said. And then I didn't speak to her again until we arrived at Mr. Muro's hotel, where we spent the next several years.

While Mr. Muro was in Manzanar, Mrs. Muro remained

in Los Angeles to manage their hotel. Hope attended a nearby Catholic school, Maryknoll, located a few blocks from their home, making Hope one of the very few people of Japanese heritage who remained in California during the war. I never bothered to ask him if he received permission from the Justice Department for Hope to remain in L.A. or whether he'd just let it slide and nobody had bothered to report the violation. Furthermore, she could have easily passed for a Chinese girl, and "Muro" isn't a common Japanese name and could easily have passed for another nationality.

Jim, the handyman, was in Room 3. A slender six-footer of German heritage and slightly hunchbacked, he was in his early sixties. With Mrs. Muro's generosity, Jim did chores around the hotel in exchange for free room and board. What I couldn't understand was why Mrs. Muro was also providing free lodging to Helen, the call girl in Room 4, even treating her as if she were her own daughter. Helen was a brunette on the attractively plump side, with a pleasant personality to match and a bosom that was the envy of any woman. She didn't appear to have very many clients, except for a fortyish Filipino man who lived on the third floor of the hotel. I often wondered why she seldom used the community toilet, until I heard from a reliable source that she had her own container in her room that she emptied once a day.

Also on the third floor were two Issei men in their early sixties. As they were both dark and slender, I often mistook Mr. Taniguchi for Mr. Watanabe and vice versa. Both were Seicho-no-Ie enthusiasts and they often visited Mother to share the philosophy of the belief while I sat on my bunk and listened. Since they conversed in Japanese, I couldn't totally comprehend what they were saying, but I got the gist of their lectures.

Mother was able to do her cooking on a small portable electric burner she kept by the sink in the corner. Mother and Edith slept on a double bed to one side, and I slept in an old canvas army folding cot—certainly not a comfortable arrangement. Perhaps that was why I ground my molars and often had nightmares of falling off a cliff. More often than not, though, I was told that I laughed in my sleep.

"What was so funny?" Edith always asked, but I could never answer because I did not know why. It was most likely because of what happened during the waking hours, since falling off a cliff in my dreams was never funny. I always woke up in a cold sweat from those imagined free falls.

"I'm going to fall all the way and find out how it feels to be dead," I said one day, determined to let it happen. But no matter how many times I tried, I could never hit the bottom. I could not die in my dreams. *How great is this!* I thought, and from then on I began to look forward to my dreams, since I could do anything I desired and never have to worry about dying.

In 1946, Edith married Stanley Yasmasaki, a tomato rancher in Tracy, California, and Mother and I suddenly had more space in our room. There were two windows next to my cot, although the view was far from spectacular. To the left and right were the red brick walls of adjoining buildings, and straight across was the white stucco wall of a more recent building on Spring Street. The hallway outside our apartment door led to the roof of Gilbert Café, and its huge round exhaust vent. We never opened our windows, since that would be an invitation to the exhaust fumes from the café. Completing the room was a dresser, a small closet, and a small table with chairs. This was our home for over three years.

The skid row of Los Angeles in the forties occupied a few select areas several blocks from City Hall, sandwiched by Spring Street on the west and Main Street on the east.

Spring Street was clean, and the buildings were immaculate, with stores on the ground floor and offices on the upper levels. There was a music shop where they sold guitars and trumpets.

That was where I purchased my first radio, a Gilfillan, in 1945.

"Hey, Hiroshi!" I shouted one day when I saw a man sweeping the gutter with a push broom, a hundred-gallon metal container on wheels at his side. Hiroshi was one of my friends from Manzanar and although he was two grades above me in school, he was a nice guy without pretense and treated me as his peer. Hiroshi was five foot five or so and slender. Behind his good-natured facade, I always felt he had an aura of determination and drive. I stared at him as he greeted me and then stopped to lean on his broom. *That's the lowest kind of job a guy can get,* I thought, but then corrected myself, *Well, at least he's not a garbage collector.*

"I'm working for the city. This is not the best job in the world, but it's the only kind of job Japs can get," he laughed.

He could have become a gardener, I thought. It was prestigious to hire a Japanese gardener to work on your yard, presumably enough to help someone move up a notch on the social ladder. Many Japanese were entering the gardening business, since Japanese gardeners had stellar reputations and were in high demand. That was the stereotype—that the Japanese were the Cadillacs of yard maintenance—but ironically one did not have to know anything about gardening to be a gardener so long as he was Japanese. That was the only prerequisite. *So why didn't Hiroshi become a gardener?* I wondered.

"I'm attending Frank Wiggins," he said. Before evacuation and after resettlement, Frank Wiggins was the most attended trade school for Nisei who wanted to learn drafting, mechanics, body- and fender-work, fashion design, and even secretarial work. The Frank Wiggins Trade School became Trade-Technical Junior College in 1954.

"I'm taking up radio repair," Hiroshi continued. I then realized why he didn't become a gardener. "Right now we're studying radio resisters."

"Hey, I got one of those cool gadgets with wheels made out

of cardboard to figure out the ohms and things like that," I said.

"I'd like to take a look at that," he said.

I gave him my address on Main Street, and a few days later he stopped by for a pleasant chat. Fifteen years later, I was elated to discover that he owned a prosperous TV repair business in Long Beach, quite a change from cleaning the gutter of Spring Street.

Main Street, only one block east of sparkling Spring Street, was like entering another world. It was lined with small shops, and starting at about three blocks south of City Hall, vagrants and winos began to occupy the sidewalks. They were neither vicious nor threatening but often bothersome.

"Hey, buddy, could you spare two bits?" they would say as they approached people walking down the sidewalk. Two bits, or twenty-five cents, seemed like the standard amount of alms for which they invariably asked. One day, a bum I'd given two bits the previous day asked me for *four* bits, giving himself a hundred-percent raise. I stupidly complied, but when I saw him later that day sitting against a building with a small brown paper bag on his lap and mumbling, I realized what a dimwit I had been in providing him with booze, which was doing nobody any good. Fresh out of Manzanar, and a country hick prior to that, I had a lot to learn amid those lost souls before I could consider myself streetwise.

On Main, there was a shoe store, a clothing store, and, three blocks south of City Hall, an army surplus store, where they sold everything from clothing to camping equipment. On the corner of the fourth block was a prestigious Farmers and Merchants National Bank, offering one percent interest on depositors' savings. It was a magnificent structure, built at the turn of the twentieth century. Past the bank was where the livelier world of skid row began to emerge, populated with even more vagrants, plus that slippery goo discharged by the winos that threatened anyone who dared trod the "colorful" skid row.

Neighboring the bank was the Muse movie theater, and two buildings south of that was the Gilbert Hotel, which Mother and I called home. There was an arcade a few doors down from our hotel, with pinball machines and air rifles with which you could take a shot at metal ducks. It was half the size of the arcade across the street, where there were more pinball machines and more rifles to take potshots at gorillas, planes, and ships, but this smaller arcade had twice as many customers, especially sailors in white bellbottom trousers. The reason soon became obvious: a beautiful, shapely peroxide blonde in a hula skirt and a bikini bra was paid to flirt with the sailors. As her grass skirt swayed from side to side with each movement, passersby could see that a G-string was her only undergarment.

This smaller arcade was lively and enticing, but I never entered it because of the sailors. The public could not distinguish a Japanese person born in America from one who had bombed Pearl Harbor, and for many, even after the war, the idea prevailed that "A Jap is a Jap, whether born here or in the land of the Rising Sun." I dared not attempt to mingle with the sailors, who may have just returned from the Pacific theater. Was I paranoid? Perhaps, but this was 1945.

Five blocks south of City Hall, the winos and the vagrants began to thin out, and after seven blocks or so, small shops could conduct their business without the interference of drunkards and the homeless.

But skid row—my skid row—was colorful and exciting. I was still attending high school, and from 4:30 to 6:30 every morning, I worked under Mr. Muro at the Muse Theatre as a janitor's helper before leaving for school. By the entrance of the theater was a life-sized picture of burlesque girls, one of whom was the legendary Evelyn West, with her "$50,000 Treasure Chest"—the amount her bosom was supposedly insured for by Lloyd's of London. Accompanying the picture was the information "Adults Only—25 Cents Admission." The movies were black-and-white films, and although they contained no sex acts, the gorgeous girls shedding their clothes, teasing the audience with each hump and bump of their butts and bosoms until they were down to their G-strings, were enough to make the customers participate in various self-indulgent sexual acts while watching the movie.

It was 4 a.m. when Mr. Muro woke me for another morning of helping him at the Muse Theatre.

At the foot of the stairwell I was careful as usual not to step on the vagrant who often claimed our entryway as his home. I was especially cautious not to step on the smelly, slippery stuff the wino had heaved up during the night.

The Muse's last show ended at 4:30 a.m., and since I had several minutes to spare, I took a seat in the back row. Within a minute, a man about fifty years old sat beside me and his hand began to traverse over my knee and thigh. I instantly pulled away, but he didn't stop, so I scooted to the next seat. He followed again and again until I was cornered against the wall. Then the screen flickered, the lights went on, and I was saved.

After waking up and herding out the remaining patrons, I began sweeping. My broom collected newspapers, wine bottles, condoms, opium spoons, and heroin needles, and I pushed everything to the center aisle, except for the newspapers, which I saved to soak up the winos' vomit and other filth. Then it was time to wash the restroom floor with the nozzle of a water hose at full blast. Soon my chores were completed and it was time for breakfast, then off on the F streetcar to Roosevelt High School.

Based on where we lived, Wanger and I should have attended Belmont High School, which was located west of Little Tokyo, but we wanted to attend Roosevelt High in Boyle Heights, where many of our Manzanar friends and classmates were enrolled, so we falsified our address as the Evergreen Hostel, temporary housing for the evacuees recently out of relocation camps.

After school we followed our usual routine. My friend Ich and I shed the coveralls we wore to auto-shop class and met Wanger and Leland at the school's entrance. A little bull session and then we were on our respective ways.

Wanger and I took the P streetcar to Little Tokyo. We went up the stairs to Wanger's family's two-room hotel space above a Chinese restaurant and spent the remainder of the afternoon listening to his Glenn Miller records. When it was time for me to walk home—only five blocks away—it was dark, and although I was usually safe, there was one incident when I turned onto the less-traveled Fourth Street and two men stepped out of the shadows between the brick buildings. One grabbed me by the arm as the other frisked me, emptying my pocket of my wallet and examining its contents. As I stood petrified, it suddenly occurred to me that aside from these two apparent thugs, there wasn't another living being in sight.

"What are you doing here?" one asked me.

"Going home," I replied.

"Where do you live?"

"417 ½ Main Street."

He returned my wallet.

"Be careful now. It's dangerous out here; you could get mugged."

I was given my wallet and set free, and as I looked back over my shoulder, the two men—plainclothes policemen, as it turned out—had already stepped back into the shadows, and the street was again dark and deserted, cold and lonely.

The following day, friends at school were full of questions.

"Was you scared, Hank?" one friend asked.

"Did they say they were plainclothesmen?" another friend wanted to know. "Did they show their badges?"

"How do you know they were cops? Maybe they *were* crooks."

Even to this day, I sometimes wonder whether they were cops or robbers, since I had no proof either way. They'd never flashed their badges, and Japanese people were commonly targeted by muggers during the postwar relocation period. Of course, if I had been a potential victim that night, I wasn't even worth the effort, since I had only a few coins in my pocket.

* * *

My long-awaited graduation from high school finally arrived, and my fellow classmates and I were ready to challenge the world...or so we thought. World War II was over, defense jobs were gone, returning GIs had filled the peacetime workforce, and jobs were now few and far between. Public sentiment toward Japanese and Japanese Americans was still cold if not hostile. Finding employment would be a challenge.

I saw an ad in the *Los Angeles Times* that California Bank on Broadway was recruiting high school graduates. Clad in a necktie and the suit Mother had bought me for graduation, I went for an interview and filled out the application form.

"How's your typing?"

"Typing? Ah...I can't type."

"Could you balance a book?"

"Balance a book? I have very good coordination, sir." My answer was innocent and sincere, not sarcastic, but the interviewer thought otherwise.

Back home, I faced the reality of what my options were. I changed into a shirt and khaki pants and jumped back into the classified section. *Maybe a carpenter or plumber's apprentice*, I thought, and followed the leads with optimism, only to find that these jobs were all unionized and, of course, for whites only.

My self-esteem was being chipped away with each interview. By the time I went for my twenty-first interview, my ego had reached rock bottom, and I was just hoping to get a dishwasher's job at a small mom-and-pop restaurant in Hollywood.

"Is the job open?"

"Yes," the restaurant owner said. He paused for a while, smiled, and continued, "I have nothing against you folks, but my customers sitting at the counter could see you when you're washing the dishes, and I might lose my customers." He sounded very apologetic.

On the streetcar home, I began to wonder how my fellow classmates were doing. There was only one way to find out: drop in to Little Tokyo. On any given day or night, somebody from Manzanar or Roosevelt High School would be roaming around First Street.

Little Tokyo, Japantown, J-Town, Buddhahead Town, Nihonmachi, or whatever else the Japanese called it, they were referring primarily to a section of Los Angeles with Japanese businesses and churches, located on First Street a block east of City Hall and extending a couple of blocks to Central Avenue.

This is where the Japanese farmers of Southern California drove to procure Japanese staples, and where people gathered every year in mid-August to join the Nisei Week festivities, which originated in 1935 with a parade and *Obon* dance. The celebration now included a carnival in a vacant lot on Second Street, set up with games and food to sate the visitors. Amid the paper lanterns and tempo of the *taiko* drums, women and girls in kimonos and men in cotton *yukata* robes swung their arms gracefully and stepped in cadence with the rhythm as they proceeded down First Street. The tradition had been carried over from Japan to offer thanks for the abundant harvest, but of course it had been put on hold with the advent of World War II, as the businesses were forced to close their doors and board their windows in the town that welcomed them for as long as half a century.

With its Japanese residents all removed to relocation camps, Little Tokyo became a ghost town, although not for long. Many of the buildings were owned by non-Japanese who were eager to rent to new tenants, which came in the form of African Americans migrating to Los Angeles from the South. The area was no longer Little Tokyo but renamed Bronze Town. With its "breakfast clubs" (so called because they were open all night until the breakfast hour), it was the liveliest place in the city, but as overcrowding became a problem (especially as vacant buildings were taken over by squatters), Bronze Town soon became a slum. Tuberculosis and venereal diseases took a toll on the residents.

In February of 1945, when people of Japanese descent were allowed to reenter the West Coast, they also returned to what had been their Little Tokyo. By the time I arrived in Los Angeles, in August 1945, Japanese people roamed the streets of J-Town, with nary a sight of the African Americans who had populated it for the three previous years.

What was behind such a speedy transition? I pondered. Many of my friends in Florin had had their neighbors or friends look after their farms while they were away and were therefore able to step right back in where they left off when the war ended, but this didn't seem to be the case in J-Town. The answer came one day while sitting in Sam's Barber Shop, located in the heart of the area. Sam's colleague, also waiting his turn, began to talk about how he was able to start his Japanese café down the street.

According to him, the property owners joined forces and procured the services of an African American who was known for his expertise in eviction and resettlement cases. They wanted his help to remove the occupants of Bronze Town. Month-to-month renters were served proper eviction notice, leases were not renewed, long-term leases and unexpired leases were bought out, and some cases were brought to court. The man followed this plan through by finding new homes and business locations for the displaced in other areas of Los Angeles—and often with improved living conditions—turning the transition into a smooth win-win situation.

One thing the new J-Town had in common with skid row was the homeless population. In J-Town, they were arriving every day from the wartime relocation centers. Japanese temples, churches, and language schools were converted to hostels, taking in as many as they could. Koyasan Temple on First Street was one of these hostels; the inside of the temple was lined with steel army cots with mattresses, neatly arranged in rows to accommodate the recent arrivals, who were allowed to stay for free until they were able to find jobs and apartments.

J-Town was shaping up to be its old self again. There was a barbershop, a dry cleaner, several chop suey houses, and a café where they served *oyako donburi* (chicken and egg bowl) for thirty-five cents. Above the shops were offices occupied by lawyers and doctors, and over the chop suey houses were hotel rooms. Japanese were returning from the camps and reopening their businesses, continuing where they had left off three years earlier. It was a dynamic community, just getting up on its feet again. This was the postwar J-Town, and the beginning of a new Little Tokyo.

I went to J-Town and began my stroll down First Street, looking for old high school friends. Sure enough, by the Taul Building, at the corner of San Pedro Street and First Street, there was my friend Ich.

"What you say, Hank?"

"Nothing much, Ich," I answered, this exchange explaining practically everything we had been doing since we'd seen each other last.

We discussed our similar situations and mutually concluded

that Japanese gardeners were making tons of money and that's what we ought to be doing.

Mother gave me $150 and Ich borrowed the same amount from his dad. With a clunker '33 Chevrolet coupe and secondhand gardening tools, we were in business, driving around Hollywood and knocking on doors with unkempt yards.

At the time, almost all the gardeners worked in the Hollywood and Beverly Hills area. Palos Verdes and Torrance were still farmlands. The San Fernando Valley was just a desert, and even North Hollywood was a mere bus stop. With a great majority of Issei and older Nisei already in the gardening business, we soon discovered that customers were scarce and the good jobs were already taken.

On the second day of our self-employment, we finally landed a five-dollar job at a corner lot on Mariposa Street. We pushed and pushed our secondhand lawn mower through the overgrown grass, but it wasn't making much difference. We took turns, mowing over the same area at least four times before it started to look even remotely properly manicured. When we started to wash off the lawn and the sidewalk, we discovered our worn hose had sprung a leak; we tied a handkerchief around the hole, and then another leak appeared. I wrapped my fingers around what holes I could, and Ich did his best to wash off the sidewalk. Five hours later, the job was finally complete.

By Thanksgiving, we had been in business for nearly four months yet due to expenses hadn't earned so much as a penny to take home. An absolute failure!

Nevertheless, I gave thanks that year since Mrs. Muro had brought us two plates filled with turkey, stuffing, and everything else to make it a complete Thanksgiving dinner. Since this was the first Thanksgiving dinner in my life, I ate to my heart's content and more. In fact, I overate to the point it became uncomfortable. By late evening the discomfort had turned to pain, and by morning I was groaning.

Mr. Muro placed his hands over my stomach and chanted prayers for several hours, followed by Mr. Watanabe, who repeated the ritual for another few hours. According to Seicho-no-Ie teachings, if I believed strongly enough, the pain would subside, but apparently I had a weak mind, since the pain only seemed to increase. I never realized overeating could cause such agony. By late afternoon on the day after Thanksgiving, I was in tears, groaning, crying, tossing and turning. Mother could not stand it any longer and called the doctor.

It was evening when Dr. Goto arrived. He placed his fingers below my ribs and pushed down.

"Does this hurt?"

"Yeah."

He pushed down on the lower left side of my stomach.

"Does this hurt?"

"Yeah."

"Does this hurt?" He pressed on the right.

"Yeah."

"It's appendicitis. Go to the Japanese Hospital, and I'll operate on you tomorrow morning." I was awed at the fact that all he did was press on three strategic points, and it didn't take him more than a minute to diagnose the problem. He had a practice in Little Tokyo prior to the evacuation and had been a doctor at Manzanar, where he performed hundreds of surgeries. This was a simple diagnosis for him.

By ten the following morning, I was on the operating table, almost unconscious, and feeling some pressure on the lower right side of my stomach.

"Wake up! Wake up!" Someone was shaking me.

I opened my droopy eyes just long enough to hear Dr. Goto say, "Here's your appendix." Pinched in tweezers and dangling above my chest was a two-inch-long cream-colored leach-like object. "You're going to be all right."

While I was recuperating at the Japanese Hospital in Boyle Heights, Ich came to visit and offered to buy me out of our gardening business for $150, my share of the investment. I agreed, but later, when I found out that he'd quit shortly afterward, I felt guilty, since the business was not worth the $150 he'd given me. His offer was purely the kind gesture of a friend.

After several weeks of convalescing, I took the only job available, a dishwasher job at Gilbert Café, located below the hotel room I shared with Mother. The customers there were not like the ones at the Muse Theatre. These were working people—no more bums, winos, and vagrants.

Two regulars used to come in at around four every afternoon. Jackie was rather short, and Dorothy had eerie bluish-green eyes. I'd first assumed these ladies were employees of the Farmers and Merchants Bank at the end of the block, since they seemed like clerical workers and the only office business in the vicinity was the bank, yet they certainly didn't dress like they worked at a bank. One day when Jackie came out of the restroom located directly behind my work area, I had to satisfy my curiosity.

"Hi. You work at the bank?" I asked.

"No, I'm across the street. Room 12. Stop by—I'll make it special for you. Three dollars."

Another girl who came to the café frequently was in such bad shape, I wondered if she was on heroin, or perhaps in a late stage of syphilis. She was sloppily dressed, had raggedy light brown hair, and walked with a wobble. As she slowly made her way toward the restroom one day, a man followed.

"What you say, pal?" He grinned as he walked past me.

When he exited the restroom some time later, still buttoning his fly, I had to ask: "Free ass?"

He nodded, smiled, took out a dollar, and paid the girl's tab at the counter. *I guess he must have been really hard up to take a chance like that,* I thought.

After calling it a day, I walked up the stairs of our hotel and ran into Helen.

"Hi, Hank. Could you lend me five dollars?"

"Sure." I sensed that somehow she knew it was my payday.

She shook my hand, scratched my palm with her index finger, winked, and whispered, "Wanna trade?" I just smiled; this offer was too close to home, and people would most likely find out if I had followed through with it. Furthermore, it was three dollars across the street, although I never patronized those girls either.

As my days as a dishwasher passed, the strong lye in the soap started to take a toll on my sensitive skin, which had turned white and begun to peel. I visited the Yamato Employment Agency and, for the price of a first week's wage for the reference, I was offered a job as a pot washer at Lawry's on La Cienega Boulevard, at the time known as Restaurant Row. The soap there was different, but my skin nevertheless worsened and began to blister, so it was back to Yamato again. Another first week's pay got me a job at California Debs, a sandal factory on Seventh and Los Angeles Streets.

It was a relief to be in a different environment. Victor, the foreman who coordinated our six-men downstairs section with the sixty men upstairs in the production area, always came to work intoxicated, but he was not a drunkard. Unfortunately for him, the boss thought otherwise.

Jake was in charge of beveling the leather soles of the sandals. Always grouchy and bossy, bit by bit, he began to irk everyone.

"What's the matter, Jake? Your wife didn't give it to you last night?" the other guys teased him.

Then there was twenty-four-year-old Harry, whose job was to sand and smooth the surface of the leather to make it receptive to glue. When Harry came in to work, he always headed for Mary, a fellow worker, grabbed her from behind, rubbed himself against her butt, and said, "How about after work?" Nosy by nature, my curiosity finally overcame me, and I said to him one day, "Hey, Harry, I thought you were married."

"Yeah, but I have five kids. I can't afford any more kids, man," implying that it was okay to have children with other women because it was at the other women's expense and not his responsibility.

Mary overheard him say this, and the remark didn't seem to sit very well with her. She picked up a strap of cowhide with both hands, yelled, "*Chingado!*" (fucker in Spanish), and whacked him on the back of one shoulder before backhanding the hide against his head. Thereafter, Mary never had to worry about anyone brushing up against her at work.

I worked at Cal Debs for eight months. Although it wasn't exactly a promotion, after Vic was terminated, I had to take over many of his chores. I was now twenty going on twenty-one. Mother and I had lived in skid row for three years going on four. I nonetheless held on to a faint glimmer of hope that it wouldn't always be this way. Moving from a janitor's helper to a dishwasher to a factory worker certainly wouldn't be considered a significant achievement, but to me it was at least a step forward and a small sign of upward mobility that I hoped would someday get me off of skid row. The way I saw it, there was but one logical choice for my next job, and that was gardening. Since I had failed in my previous attempt, I reentered the trade with mixed emotions.

With an estimated five thousand Issei, Kibei, and "older Nisei" (i.e. those who came of age before the war) gardeners in Southern California, it was definitely a crowded and competitive field, but the one consolation was that we were the only ethnic group in this occupation.

This time Mother gave me three hundred dollars, which she had saved over time from our grocery money. I bought another dilapidated Chevrolet coupe and picked up some secondhand gardening equipment. My lack of foresight became evident when I realized that there was no safe place to park a vehicle loaded with gardening tools in skid row except in an expensive underground parking lot. My head felt heavy after making the rash purchase, forcing me to lie down for a while.

Looking through the *Rafu Shimpo* newspaper the following day, I saw there was a gardening route for sale by a Kibei named Joe. Although we were total strangers, he was generous enough to give me several months to pay for the route. With his support and encouragement, I was now on my way. (And Joe later became a lifelong friend.)

These gardening jobs usually involved planting flowers, spraying weeds, fertilizing and watering the lawn, and trimming hedges. It was a complete service, requiring substantial knowledge of plants and flowers, soil and treatment, insects and fungus—all knowledge I did not possess. When I took over Joe's route, my clients' grass began to turn yellow, the stocks and snapdragons became infested with aphids, roses wilted and turned white with mildew, pansies began to die from sow bugs, gophers were pulling aralias into their holes, and devil grass began to invade the ivy. It was clear there was more to gardening than just mowing the grass, and I had to find out what to do.

I asked questions of every gardener I met, and I became good enough at the job that I continued to do it for the next few years, until I enlisted in the army. As for my parking situation, I approached my friend Rock to see if I could leave my car in front of his house every night, since he lived in a house on Bunker Hill, which was a safer area and had ample street parking on the street. Of course, he had no problem with that, and his house was only eight blocks away, which at the time was considered well within comfortable walking distance. It was also convenient, since I was visiting him on a regular basis anyway.

Every Wednesday night, Rok and I went to the newsreel

theater on Fifth and Broadway. Neither of us had a television then, so this was the only place to brush up on the week's events. Since Rok was majoring in political science in college, he was interested in world news and knew everything about politics. He even knew the names of the current senators of all forty-eight states. But we never discussed politics because that was a subject about which I was totally ignorant. I didn't even know the name of the vice president of the United States! But there was one thing we *did* discuss every week:

"Let's go to church this Sunday."

"What church?" I always asked.

"Konko Kyo Church."

"Kon-kon…what?" I had difficulty even pronouncing it. No thanks." I never considered myself a religious person.

The following week it was the same thing—"Let's go to church this Sunday"—and this continued for several months until he finally gave up, or at least I thought he'd given up. In retrospect, he'd just changed his tactics. Nonchalantly he said to me one afternoon, "You know, I don't want to go to church this Sunday because Bob and I, we're the only boys there. The rest are girls. There's nothing but girls there."

"Oh yeah?" I said. I was excited. Girls were definitely an incentive for me to go to church, and it was there that I met Kay, who later played an important role in my life.

So Rok had convinced me to attend church, and now he was trying to get me to attend Los Angeles City College, where many Nisei enrolled for two years before transferring to universities.

"Hank, there's night classes at City College now," said Rok excitedly. "Why don't you go? You receive the same credit as the day class, like us guys, except the classes are from seven to ten."

It sounded good to me, and the new semester started the following week. My friend Leland gave me a tour of the campus and took me to Holmes Hall to register. I would be attending five evenings a week, carrying fifteen and a half units; it meant completely changing my routine and lifestyle. No more Friday nights watching Japanese *chanbara* (Samurai sword fighting) movies with Leland at the Linda Lee Theater in Little Tokyo. No more Wednesday-night newsreels with Rok. After my gardening work, I borrowed the Al's Texaco gas station restroom every day as a place to clean up and change my clothes. I parked across the campus and ingested a couple of sandwiches before class, since my new suppertime was well after 10:30 p.m., and then I strolled to the library, where I invariably dozed off after reading a sentence or two in my textbook. On Mondays and Thursdays, I had to be on campus two hours earlier to fulfill the four semesters of physical education class then required for graduation, and running around after a full day's gardening work was something I wished I could do without. Nevertheless, the process itself was exciting, and I was elated I had this opportunity to attend college. At least one of the dreams I had given up so long ago was now miraculously materializing.

That said, there were a few hurdles to overcome. First among them was reading. I had never read a book from cover to cover in my life. Homework was a foreign concept. I read at a snail's pace of 168 words per minute. Those three-line quips in *Reader's Digest* were about the extent of my literary exposure; essays were beyond my abilities. Ditching, horsing around, and goofing off during my high school years had now begun to take their toll. I needed an immediate crash program on reading, writing, and study habits if I hoped to meet the rigid demands of the world of "blue books" and term papers. Taking a speed reading class solved most of my problems, and after a few years at City College, I transferred to Cal State Los Angeles, where I majored in industrial psychology and accumulated 145 units of college credit…before dropping out.

In the meantime, Mr. Muro moved to Harrington, Texas, to

operate a restaurant business with two of his friends. His wife stayed on as manager of the Gilbert Hotel, but she sold the lease about a year later, after Muro-*san* was found dead in his bathtub of having sudden heart failure at the age of sixty. Mrs. Muro sold the lease to the hotel and moved to Westchester, California, with her daughter, Hope. The new owner was an Issei lady with a daughter my age with whom I often strolled down Broadway.

Mother was in tears one day when I returned home from work. The new landlord had told Mother she didn't want her daughter going out with me, a no-good bum. We were given thirty days to vacate the premises. Fortunately, Leland, who lived on Main Street near Washington Boulevard, a few miles from downtown, knew of a vacancy in the apartment building where he lived. It was sandwiched between a Knudsen Creamery and Hank's junkyard, but it was clean and in a more desirable neighborhood, and with plenty of parking space on the street. At least seven other Japanese families lived there. Leland's parents were both dentists, and if it was good enough for them, it would be more than sufficient for me. The only drawback was that there was no garage where I could service or store my gardening equipment.

I secured our last load of belongings from the Gilbert Hotel, placed them in the trunk of the Chevy, and proceeded to our new apartment, at 2126 South Main Street. As I waited for the signal to change on Seventh Street, my clunker car sputtering and shaking and smoking, I looked in the rearview mirror and bid *sayonara* to skid row, with its arcades and burlesque shows, two-bit movie theaters and sleazy, mysterious hotels. I had always pictured the departure from skid row as a moment of jubilation, but in the moment I felt a touch of sadness, a mist of loneliness, a feeling that part of me was being left behind. Skid row, after all, had been my home for over three years—just as long as Manzanar had been. Then I noticed that my right hand was clutching a textbook, and I was reminded that even with all the adversities, tribulations, and hardships, this was still a land of great and endless opportunities, full of people to help and encourage me along the way.

Chapter Nine

THE TURBULENT YEARS

It was another perfect midsummer weekend, with not an iota of a threat that would ruin a trek up Mount Baldy. No ice or snow to impede the trail, and no sleet or rain to dampen my body or morale.

The seven-mile hike from Baldy Village could have been described as monotonous, that is until I saw smoke rising above the crest. At the summit, I joined a dozen other hikers watching two helicopters dumping water over the hot spots. The forest was on fire. One hiker with binoculars passed them around so all of us could take turns observing the fire close-up. Amid the excitement, hikers began to relate their most unusual and exciting hiking stories.

One hiker had climbed the mountains of Java and described his experience traversing the slippery algae-covered rocks of the tropics. A woman who had climbed the Himalayas told us about the night she spent in a wooden shack whose dirt floor was covered with yak droppings. For dinner, she ate yak meat, which tasted just like the droppings smelled. A hiker who went to Mexico told us how he once had to bribe the police to get out of the country. A couple who went up Mount Kilimanjaro described the wild animal safari they made as a side trip while they were in Africa.

As I listened to their stories, I was overcome with both fascination and envy, since the only time I had been out of the country save for the year in Japan after my Father died, when I was only two years old, was on a slow military transport ship to Asia as a private in the army. But at least I got that one free trip to the other side of the rock.

* * *

The contribution I made during the two years I served in the United States Armed Forces can best be described as insignificant, but it nevertheless gives me satisfaction that I served in the military with honorable intentions. The Korean War erupted in June of 1950, and all able-bodied men aged eighteen through twenty-five and without dependents were drafted. Later, all able-bodied men with dependents were also being drafted, and that meant me. Not only did I have a dependent mother, I also had a gardening business, which I would need time to sell if it came to that. I would also have to find a place to store my truck and equipment as well as a new place for Mother to live during my absence. Since I wouldn't be around to drive her, I had to find an apartment closer to markets and stores, and also near someone who could act as an interpreter if she ever needed one. If I'd waited to be drafted, I would have had to report to service as soon as I was called to duty, but by volunteering into the service, I could leave the civilian life when I was ready and prepared. And so I volunteered.

After completing basic training at Fort Ord, I was bused to Camp Stoneman, in Pittsburg, California, across the bay and over the hills from San Francisco, which was where I embarked on a troop ship. We were on our way to Korea.

There was excitement in the air as the ship slowly left the

dock, but excitement turned into solemn prayers after sea-sickness began to strike us landlubbers. Going below deck, I lay motionless on one of the tiered canvas bunks for four days. Finally, on the fifth day, Private Low and I struggled up to the mess hall, but, of course, showing we were able to walk and eat meant that we had to pull details, and the one for the day was disposing of trash into the ocean. Carrying a hundred-gallon drum of trash to the rear of the ship, we dumped it without considering the tailwind, which swept over the vessel and scattered the trash back toward us and over the entire ship. I'm ashamed to say we just left it there and walked away.

"Now hear this!" the bitch box sounded across the ship not too much later. "Whoever dumped the trash into the wind report to the ship's officer. On the double!"

I looked at Low. "Who's stupid enough to dump trash all over the ship?"

"Beats me!" he shrugged his shoulders.

Our seasickness had subsided and we were well enough to go to the upper deck to watch a movie that evening. Two fellow soldiers sitting next to us kept pulling paper and trash out of the corner and tossing it into the air, letting it float on the wind until it fell into the ocean.

"This place is filthy!"

"Yeah," his buddy remarked. "Thanks to those idiots who dumped the trash all over the ship this morning!"

"Man, those idiots ought to be court-martialed," Low joined in on the conversation with a grin.

After seventeen days at sea, it was finally time to debark at Yokohama, and also time to wake the soldier on the bunk beneath mine, who had been lying there for almost as many days, eating only when his buddy brought him food from time to time. We were greeted at the dock by a troop of Japanese dancers in kimonos who performed their *odori* as the GIs yelled with enthusiasm.

Ashore, we were sent to a huge warehouse near the dock for processing. I handed my documents to the clerk at the table. She was a Nisei girl who had come to Japan with her family from Tule Lake War Relocation Center after the war had ended and was now working for the U.S. Army. She suddenly stopped when she saw my mother's name on the document. Raising her head, she grinned. "This isn't her name, is it?"

I took a closer look and saw that her name had been mis-typed "Kuso" instead of "Kusu." We both laughed, since *kuso* is a Japanese vulgar term for feces, and I certainly didn't want my mother referred to as such, especially not on government paperwork.

Soon we were on a train to Camp Drake, near Tokyo. I was captivated by the scenery. The unpainted buildings looked just the way they did in the movies. I watched the local people stand-ing here and there along our route, waiting for some GI to toss them a cigarette.

At Camp Drake, Nisei GIs were scheduled to take a Japanese language test. On my troop ship, there were six Nisei who could understand simple Japanese phrases but not enough beyond that to serve as interpreters. I was among them. After flunking the test, we were sent to the nearby army base in Chiba, where Japanese and Korean language courses were taught. When I entered the building, I was surprised to find Bob, a friend from Manzanar, who was serving as a noncommissioned officer for that unit. At the Chiba mess hall, I discovered that the person in charge was Benny, another friend from Manzanar. I knew then that my stay there would be a comfortable one.

Benny visited me in my barrack that evening.

"Here. Wear my civvies," Benny said, handing me his sport shirt and trousers. "We'll go out and have some fun tonight!"

The terms of the occupation treaty between the United States and Japan had expired several months previously, and soldiers were allowed to wear civilian clothes off-duty.

"What kind of fun?'

"Girls, man, girls! With civvies, you can go to all the off-limit places."

"What kind of off-limit places?" I was curious.

"Yoshiwara," he smiled.

"Yoshiwara? That's the world-famous geisha district!"

I was shocked Benny would even suggest it, since I had always known him as a religious person. In an eighth-grade woodshop class at Manzanar, I remember him lecturing me on Catholicism, and after relocating to Los Angeles, we spent a month working on a farm in Stockton together during summer vacation, and he would always say, "Hank, if you're not a Christian, you're gonna go to hell, man." To him, I was a sinner. But he had changed. Now himself a sinner, he was a completely different person.

"Hey, you're okay!" I complimented him and agreed to join him in his off-limits excursion.

In the ensuing days, my classmates and I visited the Atami hot springs and the famous Ginza shopping district and its surrounding cabarets, living as though there were no tomorrow. We were destined for Korea, and even though we'd be interpreters rather than combat soldiers, there was no assurance that we'd come back alive. These could very well be our last days; we wanted every minute to be memorable, no regrets.

One day at the language school, Bob poked his head in the classroom and said, "Hank, you got a phone call."

I picked up the receiver in the office and heard a familiar voice. It was Wanger informing me that there was an opening in his office in Tokyo and I should go there for an interview. He had enlisted in the army a couple of years earlier and after attending a Japanese language school at the Presidio near San

Francisco, he was assigned as an interpreter. He was a corporal at the time but later continued to serve in the Army Reserve and eventually advanced to the rank of colonel.

The paperwork for the transfer only took one day, and soon I was in Tokyo, billeting at the NYK Building and commuting to Pershing Heights, the Eighth Army Headquarters. I was assigned to G-2, the Japanese Liaison Section, with Wanger. I would be stationed in Tokyo for the remainder of my tour.

Soon after my transfer, I received a letter from Kay, the lady friend with whom I had become acquainted at Konko Church back in Los Angeles. She informed me that Tats, our mutual friend, had a mother in Ogu, a suburb of Tokyo I was unfamiliar with.

"Where's Ogu?" I showed the address to Iizuka-*san*, a former lieutenant in the Imperial Japanese Army who was now working for the U.S. Army in our office. He wasn't sure exactly where the location was but told me he would find out.

"*Iidesuyo,*" (Don't bother) I said, since I had no intention of visiting her.

"Does the guy have any sisters?" Wanger interrupted my conversation with Iizuka-*san*.

"You know, come to think of it, I recall Tats mentioning he had a younger sister. Two years younger than me."

"Hey, Iizuka-*san*, how soon can you find out where this address is?" I was quick to change my mind, since now I had an incentive for visiting Tats's mother.

The following day, Iizuka-*san* had a detailed map and directions.

On my next day off, I bought a box of chocolate candy and rode a train to the Ogu station. I wandered around the neighborhood for hours, looking for the address, but returned without success. On my second attempt, shortly thereafter, I was able to meet Tats's sister Chiyoko, who was living with her mother.

After that, I visited them often, and one day, Chiyoko invited me to spend a midsummer day with her on a boat in Tokyo Bay. We boarded a flat-bottom boat with ten other passengers and sailed approximately one hundred yards offshore, where the boat lowered its anchor. It was the type of boat with a helmsman propelling from the rear by moving a long oar from side to side, like a fish flapping its tail.

Chiyoko and I climbed off the boat and spent half an hour picking clams where the water was shallow and the remainder of the morning basking in the sun aboard the boat. In the afternoon, we waded in the shallow water, just enjoying each other's company. At around four in the afternoon, the tide began to rise.

"We better go back to the boat," I told Chiyoko. Since she didn't appear too concerned, we took our time. The water kept rising, though, quicker than I had anticipated, and soon it was up to my waist, then above my chest, and then above her chin. I felt sure that we'd drown before reaching the boat, since neither of us knew how to swim.

"At least this is a better way to go than being shot in Korea," I said as the water rose above my head. Hanging on to her, I jumped against the sandy bottom in order to get our mouths high enough so we could get some air. The tide was rising higher and higher, and just when I had hit the point I was taking in more water than air, I saw hands reaching down to us from the boat. We were saved, but the worst was far from over.

The following day at the office, my skin started to burn and turn red from prolonged exposure to the sun and the salty air. It hurt so bad, I tried to remain as motionless as possible so I didn't have to feel my clothes rub against my body. A few days later, my arms began to swell and blister, a condition that spread to my shoulders and quads. My belly and the backs of my legs were not affected, probably because they were not exposed to direct sunlight. For several days I spent my duty hours in the office without my shirt, since the only other people in the room were Wanger and a WAAC corporal, both of whom were sympathetic to my situation. They kept a constantly lookout any approaching officers, but fortunately we didn't have any visitors during that time.

Attempting to sleep in that condition was absolute torture. I was oozing so much pus it was wetting the sheets, and after days and nights in agony it was obvious I needed medical treatment. I didn't want to go on sick call because I was afraid of being court-martialed—either accused of having gone to an off-limit locale, or perhaps just for being stupid—so I continued to bear the pain for two weeks. Eventually the pain subsided and the burns turned to scabs, and the worst part was the itching.

My first outing with Chiyoko was quite a disaster, but that didn't dishearten me enough to turn her down the next time she wanted to spend time with me. This time she invited me on a day trip to Nikko.

"So, what's at Nikko and what kind of trouble can I get into this time?" I asked in crude Japanese.

"Waterfall," she said.

"Waterfall? There are lots of waterfalls in America, like Yosemite and Niagara Falls. What's so special about Nikko's waterfall?"

"It's called Kegon no Taki and is very famous." She explained that in addition to being a spectacular sight, many lovers had jumped off the cliff into the fall, holding each other's hands to express their eternal love for each other.

"Wow!" I was impressed. "Will you jump off the cliff for me?" I asked, anticipating a romantic "Of course!" in answer.

"Sure," she said. "But you go first!"

Kegon Falls was a few hours' ride on a train from Tokyo, and the last leg of the trek was on an aerial tram with a magnificent view of the rusty autumn leaves canvassing the landscape below.

And at the top was a quaint village with small shops along the main thoroughfare. We stared at the waterfall.

I couldn't restrain my sarcasm. "The garden hose back home had more water than that!" It was October, and without regular rain, the flow was merely a trickle. A site photographer took a picture of us in front of the pitiful waterfall and later sent the picture to us for a nominal fee.

We spent the rest of the day at the village, admiring artists display their talents at skills and traditions handed down through many generations. We watched a craftsman carve a vase from a piece of tree trunk and then engrave our names and the date on the bottom. We watched a pottery craftsman mold a cup from clay, which he then let us paint before he lacquered and fired it in a wood-burning pit. The waterfall had been a disappointing dud, but our experience at the village was etched in my memory and has been cherished throughout the years.

Our next outing was Kamakura, a short distance from Tokyo.

"What's at Kamakura?"

"Buddha," Chiyoko replied.

I had attended a Buddhist Sunday school during my childhood, not because I was religious but because they passed out candies.

"We could go into Buddha's head," she added.

"Sure, you mean Buddha can go into *our* head, so we'll be indoctrinated in Buddhism." At first I was wary of her intentions, but then I discovered that she meant we could literally walk into the head of a gigantic Buddha statue at Kamakura. We followed a group of tourists up steep stairs to the top and enjoyed the view through the giant's eyes.

If all good things must come to an end, my relationship with Chiyoko was no exception. My discharge date was fast approaching, and I met her on my last day before reporting to Camp Drake for processing and embarking a troop ship back to the States. The late January chill didn't seem to affect us as we strolled down the streets of Tokyo in warm embrace. We walked through Ginza, going from store to store, and by sundown we were on its back streets, where the cabarets and bars were turning on their neon signs, making the area the brightest spot in Tokyo. We came to a small hotel, sandwiched between a cabaret and a bar.

"Shall we go in there?" I said nonchalantly. I tried to sound casual, so in case her reply was negative I could pass it off as a cheap joke.

She didn't utter a word. She gave a shy smile and nodded.

Marriage was out of the question. Chiyoko was the youngest of five children and the only one still at home. She was born in Los Angeles, had come to Japan when she was three, and her father had passed away during her childhood. Her oldest brother, in order to evade being drafted into the Japanese army, boarded the last ship to America before the attack on Pearl Harbor, her oldest sister married in Japan shortly after World War II, her second brother came to Los Angeles several years after the end of war, and her other sister married during the Korean War. That left Chiyoko alone with her aging mother, and abandoning her was definitely not an option, not even for love.

I was in a similar situation. During my tour of duty, the army was deducting half of my pay, then doubling it and sending it to Mother, who was renting a small apartment in Los Angeles until I returned home. Chiyoko couldn't leave Japan, and I couldn't stay there.

As the surrounding cabarets and bars roared with romance, fun, and laughter, it was for us one of the saddest moments in our lives; it was a farewell we thought would be forever.

After my overseas stint in the army, I returned home to Los Angeles and moved with Mother to a small one-bedroom house owned by my friend Joe. Joe gave me some of his customers to get me back into the business. I also continued my courses at

Cal State Los Angeles, using funds from the GI Bill. And in the social arena, I started dating Kay shortly after returning to the States. Several months later, the relationship developed into something more—enough for me to pop the question, "Hey, you wanna get married?"

Kay shook her head without even a moment's hesitation and follow that with an emphatic "No!" I was stunned into silence, since I was expecting an answer more like "When?" or maybe just having her jump up and down with joy. I hesitated to ask her why she had said no since I had already made an ass of myself by asking her to marry me in the first place.

I finally swallowed my pride and asked.

"Honey," she said, "I want you to be a little romantic."

Romantic? Well, we were parked on a dark, secluded street by a recreation park in a residential area of Los Angeles at one o'clock in the morning. I made sure it was in a better neighborhood than we were in the previous week when we'd seen a man standing by our car window with his fly unzipped. The 1952 Chevrolet had a bench seat, and Kay had slid over so we could huddle together in sweet embrace. How much more romantic could I get than that?

Perhaps the whole evening started out on the wrong foot with a movie at the drive-in theater. It was Hitchcock's *Rear Window*, a story about a knife, a hacksaw, and a bunch of body parts. After the movie, we went to a drive-in restaurant, where we had hamburgers and milkshakes in the car. Evaluating our date after the fact, I had to admit that perhaps the evening was far from romantic, and certainly not an ideal prelude to a romantic proposal. I apologized to Kay.

"I don't care about that," she said. "I just want to be proposed to like they do in the movies."

"Like going on my knees and holding your hands and kissing the back of your palm? That's silly!" I was adamant.

The bickering continued for the next three hours, until she finally conceded that I did not have to get down on one knee.

Purchasing an engagement ring was first on the agenda. We picked out a beautiful emerald-cut diamond ring that I could not afford. But with forty dollars as a 10 percent down payment, we were on our merry way.

When I placed the engagement ring on her finger, she said, "You know what?" I braced myself, because whenever she used that phrase, it always meant bad news.

"You know what?" she said. "Will you promise me not to ask me to have sex before we're married?" It was a shocking blow, but not the total disaster I had expected. The disappointment began to erode as I recalled an article about a recent survey that said only 19 percent of single women in the 1950s were having sex before marriage. At least she was in the majority.

As for the wedding, my ideal was eloping to Las Vegas, but Kay's version was a fancy church ceremony.

"Church wedding? Where's the excitement in that?" I asked. We finally compromised on a small church service scheduled for Easter weekend of the following year.

After the ceremony, I heard that ever familiar phrase again: "You know what?" I was sure this would be devastating news, and I preferred not to know about it. I stayed silent and kept my face expressionless.

"You know what?" she repeated with a shy smile. "I started."

"You mean the period?" I asked. She nodded with a sympathetic grin.

That was totally beyond my control, and I just had to accept it with a grin.

We departed on our honeymoon that evening. The itinerary was to go up Highway 395 along the eastern face of the Sierra Nevada, drive into Yosemite Valley, then through the Mother Lode Country (the area along the western slope of the Sierra where the gold rush of 1849 took place), and finally over to Monterey and back down the coast on Highway 1 to Los Angeles. It was a perfect plan, a dream of a honeymoon (save for that glitch of the latest "You know what").

"You know, there's an old gold mining town called Columbia in the Mother Lode Country, and according to my geography teacher, it only missed becoming the capital of California by one vote. Can you believe Columbia would have been the capital instead of Sacramento?"

"Oh," Kay commented. That part of California history didn't appeal to her, perhaps because she had been born and raised in Tacoma, Washington, whereas I was born and raised near Sacramento, not far from the Mother Lode Country. I've always said if I could pick a place to die, I would choose somewhere in Gold Country, whether in the mountains or the desert.

If one goal of honeymooning is to get away from people and civilization, we certainly attained our objective. Driving through the desert, we were approaching the small town of Mojave when we saw a neon "Vacancy" sign appear on the dark horizon. We parked the car in the unpaved lot, checked in, and went to our room. What we found was far from being a honeymoon suite. The floor was covered with linoleum that was torn in places, and the bathroom was shared with the room next door, separated by doors with a sliding latch for privacy. At least the adjoining room was vacant that evening.

The following morning, we continued northward along the eastern Sierra to Red Rock Canyon, a spectacular area surrounded by colorful mountainsides. It was there we heard an announcement over the radio that the road into Yosemite Valley from the east was closed due to an early May snowstorm. We would have to alter our itinerary.

"Hey, no problem. We'll backtrack a few miles, drive up Highway 49 through the Mother Lode Country, and get into

Yosemite from the west. This will make our honeymoon a little more memorable," I said.

We drove from Fresno to Mariposa, the southernmost old mining town of Gold Country. There was nothing but dried grassland along the way, and as the car went up and down the rolling terrain, *poof, poof, poof,* white smoke began to come out the exhaust, and finally the engine died and the car came to rest.

"Do you want me to call a tow truck?" a passerby asked.

"Thank you, but that's okay," I said, confident that this wasn't anything serious and completely unaware that the trouble was actually something beyond a simple roadside repair.

"Would you like me to get you a tow truck?" the next passerby asked. It had been over half an hour since the previous car had passed by, and as I internalized that we were far from civilization, I decided it was better to get some help before we lost our chance and ended up spending the night in the car out in the boondocks.

We sat in our car while the tow truck hoisted it by the front bumper and then rumbled us off to a garage in Mariposa, where the mechanic diagnosed a damaged timing gear and then immediately began to disassemble the front end of the car to get to the engine. Since the mechanic did not have the correct part on hand, he was unable to repair us that day, forcing us to spend the night in town. Fortunately, there was a motel and a general store nearby, so we picked up a loaf of Weber's Bread, a package of Oscar Mayer bologna, and couple bottles of Coke for a honeymoon dinner in our motel room.

The next day, the mechanic drove fifty miles to Fresno to purchase the repair part, and it was dusk by the time he returned, which meant another night in Mariposa. During my bachelorhood, I often daydreamed about being marooned on a desert island with the girl of my dreams and what a wonderful life it would be. Mariposa was somewhat like a desert island—fresh air, beautiful spring weather, away from the crowds—but I began to have second thoughts about that dream after being cooped up in a motel room for two days and two nights with nothing to do. Since we'd lost those two days, we had to scrap the plan of visiting both Yosemite and Columbia, but as a small consolation we visited an old courthouse in Mariposa, the oldest active courthouse west of the Rockies. It certainly was not a conventional honeymoon, but for two people in love, it was a honeymoon we cherished and remembered, often with a chuckle and a hug.

A year later, we purchased a frame house in Los Angeles. It had a backyard where Mother was able to grow different varieties of chrysanthemums and cacti, and also continually pull out the devil grass that constantly invaded our dichondra lawn. For the first time in the fourteen years since leaving her farm in Florin, she was able to work with Mother Earth again.

Several years later, Mother left us, sailing off to Japan both to visit Father's resting place and to spend a few years with Ben, who was living in Osaka. She chose to board a Japanese cargo ship, since it allowed the passengers to dine with the captain and crew, who were Japanese. When Miharu came to send Mother off on her voyage, she noticed the Verona Clipper on Mother's dresser. When we had arrived at Manzanar, Mother had requested that her steamer trunk, which had been kept in storage at a federal warehouse facility, be shipped to us in camp. The Verona Clipper, which had been resting at the bottom of the trunk, had been in Mother's possession ever since, once again with nothing to embrace except for her broken dreams. Miharu picked it up, perhaps remembering her childhood years, when it was kept on Father's roll-top desk.

Since Miharu was an avid collector of antiques as well as a person with strong sentimental attachment, Mother must have felt that Miharu should be the keeper of the vessel. Mother gently cuddled the Clipper as though she were embarking on her own last voyage and was saying farewell to this piece of her past for the last time. Then she handed it to Miharu. Perchance Mother somehow knew that in two years she would pass on in Ben's arms and join Father at his resting place, never to return to America or touch the Verona Clipper again.

Meanwhile, I quit gardening and opened a jewelry store in West Los Angeles, which could only be described as a two-year fiasco. After that, I worked as a Fuller Brush man, the owner of a mail-order business, and as a life insurance agent, all failures in themselves. One day I realized I had only twenty-five cents in my pocket.

As I parked the car in front of a neighborhood convenience market, I rolled the quarter between my fingers in contemplation. It was my last coin, and I felt I should spend it wisely and for a worthy cause. By then, I was in my thirties and the father of two children. Karen was three years old and Bruce less than one. As an insurance man—my latest occupational incarnation— the fact that I had no sales brought havoc and destruction upon my family and morale, and it was becoming evident that I had been on the road to self-destruction for some time.

A quart of milk for my kids would cost nineteen cents, and a pack of cigarettes is twenty-four cents, I thought, *but I haven't had a smoke all morning.* It felt like one of the greatest decisions of my life. Would I abandon my children and let them starve while I blew smoke rings? I had never lacked in self-esteem, but for once I began to wonder if all along it had only been pseudo self-esteem, conjured up in my vulnerable mind. If there is such a thing as a devil inside me, it was making its appearance known in that moment. I entered the market, put the quarter on the counter, and said, "Marlboro."

Back in the comfort and seclusion of my car, my hands began

to tremble as I lit my Zippo and took the first puff. I felt my face turning red and a cold sweat sweeping over my forehead and chest. Soon my shirt was soaking wet. Yes! Apparently I would let my kids go to hell while I indulged in self-satisfying pleasures. That was who I'd become; it was an undeniable truth! I sat for an hour in disgust, hating myself and thinking of some punishment that would make everything right.

I drove home and said, "Hey, Kay, I'm going to start gardening again." I changed my clothes and drove to a lawn mower shop.

I asked the shop proprietor (whom I knew) if he could sell me a Trimmer power mower, a Power Trim power edger, a hose, and some hand tools, letting me pay for them over the next three months. He agreed, and by that afternoon I was in North Hollywood, placing an ad in the local newspaper, knocking on doors, and mowing lawns.

By working seven days a week until sundown, it took only three weeks to build up a full route and lose twenty pounds. It was without a doubt self-inflicted punishment, but with each drop of sweat and each ounce of weight lost in the hundred-degree summer temperatures, it was as though the evil and poison were slowly draining out of me. My self-esteem had dwindled to almost nothing during my years of failure after failure, and finally I was becoming financially stable. In two years, we were able to purchase a newer and larger home in Gardena.

I was itching to start another business, but I temporarily suppressed my yen and settled for buying two income properties in Gardena, which I then sold to start a printing business several years later.

During that time, we had our third child, Janette, and couple years later, Michelle was born.

Michelle was only three years old when I decided to take the family out to spend a day in the desert, a field trip I'd hoped they'd never forget.

"Okay, kids, we're going out to the Mojave Desert today to look at some fish," I said. I watched them look at each other, confused and in agreement that they had a loony father. I was planning to show them something they had never seen, something they never even knew existed: fish in the middle of the desert.

We rumbled along in our green Rambler station wagon. We had been on the road for several hours, and restlessness was in the air.

"Are we there yet?" Karen asked as we bumped along a dusty dirt road. I couldn't answer her because, truthfully, I was lost.

"Mommy, it's hot," Michelle whined.

"I'm hungry," Janette complained.

"How far, Dad?" Bruce asked.

"Oops! I took a wrong turn. I think it's supposed to be that-a-way," I said as I made a sudden U-turn. Without road signs to guide the way, I was depending on pure luck and prayer to get us where we needed to go.

"Oh no! Not again!" Kay remarked as she desperately attempted to fan away the dust with a road map. Her usual controlled temperament began to erode as the desert heat and dust began to take its toll on her and our passengers.

This is a trip they'll remember forever, I told myself.

"What are we looking for?" Karen asked, perhaps thinking she'd heard me wrong the first time. We were surrounded by sagebrush and creosote plants, with not a sign of water, not even a trace of humidity in the atmosphere.

"Fish," I said, and the station wagon was filled with cynical laughter. To me, however, it was no joke. This was going to be a lesson in survival—survival of what were called pupfish in the remote corner of this desert. I though the inspirational lesson of the pupfish could help the children mature a little, become better able to embrace the hardships, the failure, the poverty, and the mishaps of life rather than succumb to them. For if fish can survive in the arid, dusty, desolate land of the Mojave Desert, how much easier for mankind to survive the discomforts of civilization, however dismal it may seem at times.

Finally, we were there! The area was enclosed by a tall chain-link fence, and beyond the fence, under what appeared to be a flat boulder of either granite or sandstone (for some reason, I can never distinguish between the two) was a pool of crystal clear water, apparently extending into a small underground cavern. Although we couldn't see them, we knew the pupfish were there because the UCLA research department's sign said so.

We never did spot an actual fish in the desert, and in retrospect, it was just a dusty, bumpy, hot Saturday excursion into the Mojave Desert without any real aesthetic or educational value. Besides, most people had never heard of a pupfish back then, and even if they saw one, they wouldn't be able to distinguish it from an ordinary guppy. But at the time, when I was revved up in parenthood mode, I never missed an opportunity to overemphasize the importance of building strong moral character in my children, even when that led to outlandish behavior and wild goose chases through the desert on my own part.

Now, many years later, I often reminisce about those adventures, recalling vivid pictures of our family on weekend field trips on desert roads, caged in a station wagon without an air conditioner. They are fond memories that I relive time and again and cherish dearly. Perhaps this is what parenthood is all about: sharing the joys and laugher as well as the sorrows and despair, through the good times and the lean years, and always being able to look back on those moments decades later with a chuckle and a smile.

* * *

Back atop the Mount Baldy summit, we watched the helicopters continue to douse the hot spots. The scent of burnt brushes was creeping up the slope.

There are three major trails up to Mount Baldy summit: Devil's Backbone to the north, Ski Hut Trail, and Mount Baldy Trail from Mount Baldy Village. For a while, Devil's Backbone seemed impassable due to smoke and fire, but within an hour or so, the main blaze seemed to be under control, and the occasional flare-ups were immediately drenched by the helicopters. The excitement was over, but my fellow hikers and I continued to sit together in the stone shelter shaped like an oversized fire pit, basking in the sun as a cool breeze whooshed past us. The others kept telling their best stories from their travels to the four corners of the earth. I sat and listened, for I felt I had no tale to tell.

* * *

Although I was overseas with the army, which may sound thrilling and dangerous, I was a lowly private assigned to an office in Tokyo, at the bottom of the totem pole and responsible for little more than hand-cranking the ditto machine and managing other simple tasks like collating and stapling.

Ditto machines were the precursor to modern copiers, and when the duplicating revolution erupted in the early 1970s, I was intrigued.

In February of 1973, I attended a franchise show at which instant printing was introduced. The show was followed by a printing exposition further showcasing this new technology in a brand new industry that was transforming a formerly labor-intensive task into a wonder of technology.

Perhaps it was my experience cranking the ditto machine during my army service that led me to opening an instant print shop.

"That's a tough business. You're not gonna make it, man." My friend Benny was very explicit. Other friends and acquaintances were polite and tried to camouflage their feelings, although their thoughts on my foolish venture always appeared in their body language.

I nevertheless launched a printing shop in Gardena called Presto Prints. While Kay took orders during the day, I mowed lawns to supplement our income and then worked at the shop from late afternoon to evening, and often into the morning hours. Since instant printing was still in its infancy and I had much to learn, jobs that should have taken only minutes always stretched out over hours.

At the end of our first year of business, we were in the red and had reached a point of no return; we could not quit since we were tens of thousands of dollars in debt, and so I continued with my eighteen-hour-day work regimen, not by choice but necessity. I called it a "learning period"—a costly learning period that saw tons of paper sifted into the dumpster because of mistakes and general incompetence. The second year appeared promising, though; we broke even. By the third year, a little profit began to emerge—enough to begin phasing out my lawn work. From that first lowly job of duplicating, collating, and stapling in the army office in Tokyo, I grew a successful printing business that lasted for thirty-two years, until my retirement.

It was during this period that my sister Miharu passed on. Yosh and Miharu owned a carnation nursery business in East Palo Alto and later sold the business to retire in Fremont, near the Bay Area. When I attended her funeral, I spent the night in her home and noticed she kept the Verona Clipper in her work room. It was one of Miharu's most treasured possessions, placed on a dresser by the entrance to the room where she spent hours every day pursuing her craft hobbies. The Clipper was always beside her.

Now tarnished black with only small spots of copper showing through, the Verona Clipper was again packed away in a box. Its life in our family had spanned more than eighty years, and two generations. Would the next journey be across continents and the seven seas, or to a dark attic where it would be forgotten?

Yosh carefully placed a blank shipping label on the box and began to address it with a felt-tipped pen: "Hank Umem…"

Today, the Verona Clipper rests on a shelf above my desk, holding the books Mother had bought me during my teen years. On the bottom of one of the bookends is a large ink blot marring the original green felt padding. As I gaze at the smudge, I can vividly visualize Father sitting at his roll-top desk, picking up a pen to make an entry in the cloth-covered ledger, and accidentally knocking the ink bottle across the desk, the dark blue ink slowly seeping into the base of the Clipper.

Chapter Ten

SLUM VENTURE

When I bumped into Dave and Dorothy on Mount Baldy Trail, they explained why I hadn't seen them the previous couple of weeks. They'd broken an axle on their four-wheel-drive Trooper in the backcountry. Any trail that breaks an axle would have to have been an exciting trek, I figured. I once bent a drive shaft when crossing a dry river bed strewn with boulders and had to drive home on the freeway at twenty-five miles an hour, with passing motorists shouting cusses and giving me the finger. It was a lesson well learned about maneuvering over rocky terrain. My only consolation was the free six-hour massage I got driving home in a shaky truck.

When I met up with Dave and Dorothy on the trail the following week, Dorothy handed me some literature and a topographic map of Bridge Mountain. It is only seven thousand feet in elevation but held the promise of adventure.

Only about forty miles from downtown Las Vegas, the ornate neon spectacle of the city is replaced by the vistas of the surrounding Red Rock Canyon. After entering Lovell Canyon and driving up several wrong jeep trails, I finally came to what looked like the right one. The trail had its share of holes and humps but the thing that stood out was the angle of its rise, which appeared steep enough to topple a vehicle onto its side and toss it into the gorge below. Tensely navigating the tilted terrain, I soon arrived at a wash about three feet deep and fifteen feet wide, an array of boulders covering its irregular surface. I stepped out of the truck and appraised the area. One large boulder stood out among the others. It had a patch of black on its protruding tip and then an oil drip mark a few yards further down. Someone's oil pan may have been damaged on the rock. It was a horrifying thought.

I've often heard the phrase "rocky marriage," and indeed it can be like traversing rocky terrain. You have to tread the field very slowly and cautiously, maybe even having to call it quits when the going gets too rough. Unfortunately, I knew all too much about this from personal experience.

* * *

In the beginning, my marriage to Kay was indeed one of the happy segments of my life. We had four children to keep us busy, and the kids were certainly instrumental in keeping our marriage together. As they grew and began to pursue their own dreams, however, Kay and I also began to go our separate ways, and our marriage was on the fringe of entering a serious rough patch.

"Happy twenty-fifth anniversary!" The lights turned on and our kids and relatives applauded and shouted their congratulations as Kay and I entered the house one evening after returning from work. It was a surprise party with cake and presents, and although it was appreciated, it was a bittersweet moment: sweet that they were acknowledging our seemingly happy marriage of twenty-five years, but bitter in that we would someday soon have to announce that we were calling it quits. Seeing how elated everyone was, but knowing the dismal future of relating the bad news, I did my utmost to conceal my true emotions as the party continued on into late evening.

One Sunday morning, I heard that ever familiar "Honey, you know what?" I waited for her to continue, anticipating more bad news. "I lost my diamond," Kay said as she extended her left hand toward me, her fingers spread apart. I looked at her ring finger and saw four prongs with a blank space inside. "It must have fallen into the laundry tub," she added. I disassembled the drain trap, hoping the stone would be resting there, but to no avail.

"It must have gone down the drain," I said as I shrugged my shoulders.

She shrugged her shoulders too and grinned. I held on to her arms as we puckered up for a little tap on the lips. We were both aware that our marriage was fizzling out. The emerald-cut diamond that had disappeared down the drain and that was once was so precious and dear to us was only a prelude to the future of our marriage.

By the summer of 1982, the day of reckoning had arrived. Kay was in Seattle with her sister for Labor Day. I was deciding what to do over the long holiday weekend by myself when a mutual friend phoned and said that Chiyoko's mother, who had returned to the United States in the early sixties with Chiyoko, was seriously ill and her days were numbered. This came as a surprise, since I hadn't seen either of them in decades. Nonetheless, I paid them a visit. Chiyoko's mother was unable to move freely and didn't recognize me. By the following spring, she had passed on, and Kay and I were separated. Eventually, Kay and I ended our marriage with an amicable divorce, and we continue to maintain respect and consideration for each other and our mutual friends.

Having reconnected with Chiyoko, we started spending

time together more often. One time I was at her apartment, I noticed the curios she kept on the fireplace mantle. One was a wooden vase carved out of a tree trunk and another was a cup molded in clay that we had painted together that day we visited the quaint little village of Nikko. Perhaps there was a chance to rekindle the flame we had extinguished on the back streets of Ginza so long ago.

During the summer of 1992, Chiyoko accompanied me to the fifty-year reunion of Sierra School, where I had been enrolled before being sent to Manzanar. We went in the motor home I had bought and extended our trip to Lake Tahoe, Virginia City, and Reno.

"Shall we go in?" I asked Chiyoko as we came to a stop in front of a quaint wedding chapel.

She nodded with a grin, and there in front of a minister, we exchanged our marriage vows, fulfilling a dream that had been snuffed out in 1954 while in the army, exactly thirty-eight years previously.

* * *

I stood in the middle of the rocky wash wondering whether to turn back or proceed up to the Bridge Mountain trailhead. There was a third option, too—park the truck where it was and hoof it up to the trailhead—but when I noticed three sets of fresh tire tracks coming up on the other side of the wash, I decided to drive on since it was obvious that others had made it farther up the trail.

Having passed through the wash and arrived at the trailhead without any mishap, I found a red Jeep Cherokee parked in the small lot in front of the trailhead. Donning my waist pack and water bottles, I scanned the landscape, which promised what appeared to be a very easy hike. And it was indeed easy, up until the trail ended abruptly at a rocky crag. I saw cairns, or ducks, as they are often called, that indicated the trail was nearby, but I could not find any evidence of a path. I wandered back and forth until a group of hikers coming down the mountain pointed me to a gigantic boulder about a hundred feet high with a deep vertical crevice down its surface.

"You mean I have to climb that?" I looked at the crack between the rocks.

"Well, it's isn't as bad as it looks," they assured me.

My route was a space about two feet wide between two rock walls. The trick was to put one foot against each side and waddle up like a duck on a vertical incline. But they were right. The crack was scalable, although rather scary, but I did it.

The trail led up to the top of a natural sandstone bridge, my final destination. At that point, my concern turned to whether I would be able to get back to my truck and drive out to the main road before dark. I've never driven a jeep trail at night, and definitely didn't want my first time to involve crossing a boulder field. Traversing it in daylight had been challenging enough.

* * *

Living through a rocky marriage with Kay had been tense, but there were challenges yet to come as Chiyoko and I began our new life together. I at least qualified to purchase a home with little or no down payment, since I had never used my GI Bill to purchase property up to that time, but I was broke and heavily in debt, and at fifty-five years old, I only had ten years until retirement age to become financially solvent.

I concluded that getting into real estate would be my best approach for acquiring quick cash. But as happened in most of my ventures, there was a glitch: I didn't have much money to get started. Fortunately, through bidding in an auction, I was able to purchase income properties in Los Angeles, Torrance, and Inglewood. The properties were in blighted neighborhoods that the mortgage holder could not sell on the regular market, and they came with the bonus of gangs, graffiti, narcotics, and lawsuits.

One Memorial Day weekend, I stepped out of my front door and a man asked my name, handed me a set of papers, and then immediately turned around and walked away. The paper was titled "Summons," and my first thought was that this was definitely an effective way for an advertisement to attract my attention. Then I got to the section that read "YOU ARE BEING SUED BY PLAINTIFF, (JANE DOE)," followed by the seal of the Superior Court of Los Angeles County.

I read through ten pages of legal jargon I did not understand. It mentioned my rental unit on 36th Street in Los Angeles and my negligence in maintaining the property. The eleventh page concluded with "COMES NOW the Plaintiff, (JANE DOE) and pursuant to Code of Civil Procedure Section 425.11, sets forth the Statement of Damages as follows: (1) Medical Specials—$19,048.50 (2) General Damages—$100,000.

Could this be some kind of a gag? I was perplexed. I went to the address and noticed the broken and uneven concrete sidewalk, the result of a huge tree root that was there long before I purchased the property. Had the plaintiff tripped and fallen?

I read over the summons again and became even more concerned when I noticed that the case was assigned to the Central District of the Los Angeles Supreme Court and would involve a jury trial lasting four to five days. I called my insurance company, which immediately hired a lawyer to answer the summons and make countercharges.

A couple of weeks passed, and during that time I realized the incident had happened during a period I was not covered by insurance, due to a freak mix-up. Should I keep quiet and let the insurance company handle this? Or should I admit up front that I was not insured at the time of the incident? Either

I could remain silent and possibly walk away free, albeit as a dishonest person, or I could inform the insurance company of the error and face the possible $119,048.50 liability as an honest man with a clear conscience. I decided that I would rather have a clear conscience, so I contacted my insurance company.

When I notified the insurance company of the discrepancy, they treated me with sympathy and forfeited all costs they had incurred up to that time and agreed to transfer all legal papers to my attorney. My lawyer studied the case and began to look for precedent, but he was only able to find a weak one.

"Let me try buying her out," he said. I listened as he phoned the plaintiff and tried to persuade her lawyer to accept our as-yet-undetermined monetary offer, but the plaintiff declined.

A rough road stretched out ahead of me. I signed a contract agreeing to pay my lawyer for his services: $350 per hour for an estimated minimum of thirty hours plus a $1,700 retainer fee. Either way, whether I won or lost the case, I was a loser.

To keep my mind off my problems, I began to take a more strenuous fourteen-mile trail up Mount Baldy instead of my usual ten-mile hike. Supplementary Sunday bike rides of forty-five miles from Torrance Beach to Will Rogers Beach helped further ease my tension, but the suspense of the suit always lingered in the back of my mind.

I was soon served with a sixteen-page document from the plaintiff's lawyer titled "Interrogatories and Demand for Production of Documents." The barrage of questions was essentially a few basic questions phrased in many different ways, principally whether I maintained the tree in the parkway that had buckled up the sidewalk, and whether I had reported the hazardous condition to the city. I admitted that I was aware of the danger but hadn't reported it to the city. "Negligence" was the key word in all of this, and it seemed they had a very strong case against me. My lawyer's confidence was beginning to wane.

It was mere coincidence that I happened to pick up the *Rafu Shimpo* one day in August to see what was new in Nikkei society. I was shocked to see an article about Nisei women in Little Tokyo who were occasionally tripping on a section of sidewalk that had been pushed up and broken by the roots of a magnolia tree in the parkway. After all the predictable red tape, the city finally agreed to repair the sidewalk, and there next to the article was a photo of a city crew working on the concrete. The article made it clear that the municipal government was fully responsible for the maintenance of the sidewalk, not the nearby property owners.

Sending that article to my lawyer was enough to turn the case in my favor, and a date was set for an arbitration hearing, possibly eliminating the need for a jury trial. Three days before the hearing, good news arrived: a preliminary out-of-court settlement by the city and possible dismissal of the case for me. The case was eventually dismissed.

Those twelve months I spent stressing out about the $119,000 liability were behind me, and I sometimes wonder with both bewilderment and gratitude that it turned out so favorably.

In that instance, honesty definitely paid off, but when one of my tenants vacated his property leaving two pit bulls tied to a post in the backyard on a short chain and without food or water, I learned that sometimes dishonesty is the better policy.

When I approached the dogs, I was nipped by one of them, although luckily his teeth did not penetrate through my Levi's. I had previously been warned by the tenant that his dogs would bite, and I once saw a small terrier lying dead in that same backyard, apparently killed by one of the pit bulls. The dogs kept lurching toward me against their chain, making me extremely cautious and afraid to even approach them with food or water.

I called the local animal control the following day, but I was reminded that the city ordinance stated that the landlord is responsible for property left by a tenant for fifteen days, including dogs.

"But the dogs are vicious, and I can't even go near them to feed them," I explained. "Besides, the dogs don't even have licenses." The only response I got was that I must feed and care for them.

Things didn't sound right, so I called the city attorney's Criminal Division, which in turn referred me to the city attorney's Housing Enforcement Department, which referred me to the Los Angeles Housing Department. These dead ends led me to the Apartment Owners Association, the police, and finally the American Society for the Prevention of Cruelty to Animals (ASPCA), which recommended that I call animal control.

"But that's where I started!" I said.

After this arduous yet futile attempt to remove two vicious dogs from my rental unit, I grunted in anger that this was a good example of bureaucracy, using the *Merriam-Webster* definition as "the administration of government through departments and subdivisions managed by sets of appointed officials following an inflexible routine. See also RED TAPE." If I had consulted the dictionary first, I wouldn't have wasted my time on this hopeless treadmill.

Contacting all those city agencies must have done some good, however, since an animal control officer arrived the next day. She was very pleasant and left me with this wise advice: Just call the office and say you found a stray dog and don't know the owner, and they'll come pick it up right away. Dishonesty was apparently an effective instrument in weaving through bureaucracy.

I was able to cope with various tenant problems for many years, until the day that proverbial straw finally broke this camel's back. One of my rental units in Inglewood had two two-bedroom homes on a lot. The tenant in the rear house called and wanted his leaky kitchen faucet fixed. When I arrived, I noticed the security door of the front house was ajar, and upon closer examination, I saw that the metal door was bent as though it had been pried open with a crowbar. The solid wooden door was hanging loose on one hinge, and the door jamb was broken in several places. Inside, the bureau drawers had been removed and clothes were scattered all over the bedroom. In the kitchen, a fresh steak sat out on the counter, ready to put in a frying pan. My guess was that the house had been raided by the police and the tenants had escaped in a hurry.

I made my way back through the mess and proceeded to the rear house. As I approached the door, I smelled marijuana.

"Hey, this is Hank. You in there?" I shouted.

"Yeah, come on in," came a voice.

When I entered the living room, the tenant was lying on the sofa holding a joint between his index finger and thumb.

"Hey, how's it going?" I asked.

"How you doing, dude?" he greeted me. "Man, this is good stuff," he added as he puffed on the grass.

"Where did you get the stuff?" I asked.

He explained that he'd bought it from the tenant in the front house, who was growing the weed in his bedroom. I decided then and there that it was time for me to call it quits in this business. I liquidated my holdings and thought I was free, but little did I know the worst was yet to come. In April, Uncle Sam had the last laugh when I had to write checks totaling $150,000 in taxes.

Looking back, I am appalled at how often I've led myself into ill-fated affairs when there are far more enjoyable things in life. There's the whiff of fresh morning air, the scent of pine trees, the rhythmic whishing and splashing of mountain streams, and meeting our friends—the black bears, the deer, even the rattlers—along the trail and acknowledging they have just as much right to this planet as we humans. There's the spectacular vista from atop a mountain, looking down onto the white blanket of cloud below or into a valley painted with lakes and streams and greenery. Above everything else, there was always one challenge I longed to undertake: making it to the top of the Big One, Mount Whitney.

Chapter Eleven

BLACK OUTHOUSE BEACON

"If you can make this, you can make it up Whitney," Dave said to me while we were relaxing atop Mount Baldy.

"Yeah, Hank, you shouldn't have any trouble," Dorothy, his wife, added.

"Well," I hesitated. I had made a vow to climb Mount Whitney one day, but as an elderly hiker, my hopes weren't very high, despite the successes I'd had on lower peaks.

"You could always go as far as you can and then come back," Dave laughed.

It sounded like a joke, but the more I thought about it, the more it made sense. His words lingered in my mind.

Just to satisfy my curiosity, I drove to Lone Pine, where the asphalt Whitney Portal Road begins its ascent to Whitney Portal and from there to the trailhead. Lone Pine is only about ten miles from Manzanar, situated at the foot of Mount Williamson. Williamson is the second tallest peak in California, and although it's only 116 feet lower than Whitney, hardly anyone has heard of the former, whereas the latter is known worldwide.

About 125 miles north of Mojave on Highway 395 is the

town of Lone Pine. From there, for the first time, the three crests of Mount Whitney are visible behind the mountains in the foreground. Whitney Portal Road veers west for thirteen miles from Lone Pine toward the Sierra Nevada Range through the Alabama Hills and to the Whitney Portal parking area, where there is a campground and a store open during the hiking season that serves hearty breakfasts and hamburgers at lunch.

Since the distance from the Whitney Portal trailhead to the summit is almost eleven miles, with an altitude gain of slightly over six thousand feet—a formidable task—I broke the hike into seven segments in my mind, so I could concentrate on hiking one short section at a time rather than trying to tackle the entire trek in one sweep.

The first segment was from Whitney Portal at over eight thousand feet to Lone Pine Lake, a distance of two and a half miles and an elevation gain of two thousand feet.

Leaving Whitney Portal, I trudged, huffed, and gasped for air through the pine and chaparral terrain up a pulverized granite and sand trail (often referred to as a "smooth trail"). After about an hour and a half, I finally reached the end of the first stretch of my hike: Lone Pine Lake. Finding a large flat boulder by the lake, I spent the remainder of the day there basking in the sun, realizing what a fool I was to even imagine the possibility of getting to the top of Mount Whitney. At least I made the first segment, I consoled myself.

Two years and three months had elapsed since I'd begun climbing the local peaks. Having chatted with scores of veteran hikers, their comments were always the same: "You could make Whitney!" The only words to the contrary were in my own voice: "There's no way!"

Remembering the old adage "It's better to have tried and failed than not to have tried at all," I finally made a firm decision to make my first serious attempt to climb Whitney—the whole thing—in October of 1998.

I left after work on a Friday evening, and I arrived at Whitney Portal at 10:30 that night. My excitement and the frigid temperature kept me awake well past midnight, and what little rest I did get was frequently interrupted by the young hikers who pulled in behind me and then stayed up talking into the early morning hours. I probably got a scant hour and a half of sleep before hitting the trail at 4:30 a.m.

"Splash!" I hadn't realized the rock I'd stepped on was covered with ice, and now I was standing in an icy stream.

"Hey, I like your style," a hiker joked as he watched me through the ordeal.

Soon my Levi's were stiff like a pair of stovepipes, frozen solid from the cold. Perhaps this is one of the reasons experienced hikers wear synthetic materials rather than cotton.

It was still dark at this point, and as I resumed the hike, guided by my powerful halogen flashlight, suddenly poof! the batteries were dead, after less than an hour of use. My hands were numb (I didn't have gloves), and the simple task of changing batteries became an impossible chore. I waited for the next group of hikers to catch up so they could assist me.

Noticing my bare hands, one hiker handed me a pair of gloves. "I have extras," she said.

By daybreak, Lone Pine Lake was at last in sight. It was the milestone marking the first segment of trek, which I had only barely accomplished the first time I'd tried it, during daylight hours.

The next section was from Lone Pine Lake to Outpost Camp, a distance of one mile with an elevation gain of four hundred feet. The scenery was spectacular and the trail only became challenging as it began to hug the southern cliff of Mount Thor. After another half an hour, tents and campers began to appear as the trail descended into Outpost Camp. It was a relief to be headed down, and I dared not think about having to go uphill on the return trip.

It was a fairly easy trail from Outpost Camp to Mirror Lake, a distance of half a mile with an elevation gain of three hundred feet. Approaching the lake, I stopped when I heard the roar of water. It was a stream about thigh deep with a few huge boulders exposed. Since diving into the icy waters was not an option, I made sure the soles of my shoes were dry so I would have traction as I crossed the water using the boulders as stepping-stones. Holding my breath the whole way, I made it to the other side without incident. From there, Mirror Lake appeared on the right, pristine and beautiful, deserving of its name. Recovering from overuse in the past, the lake was off-limits to campers.

When I saw the trail traversing huge boulders and then vanishing into a forest of rocks instead of pine trees, I knew tough hiking was ahead on the way to Trailside Meadows, thankfully only a mere mile away over a seven-hundred-foot elevation gain. In less than an hour, I was there. With its lush green vegetation and the stream running through the glen, it was a beautiful sight to behold.

The next part of the trail—from Trailside Meadows to Trail Camp—was over boulders and pulverized granite. It was a short stretch of slightly over a mile with a gain of seven hundred feet, but at almost twelve thousand feet above sea level, it was strenuous and challenging. It took me nearly an hour to reach my marker for the end of this section: a black outhouse structure, for liquid waste only, since a "poop bag" was issued to hikers for carrying out solids, which could be disposed of in a receptacle at the trailhead. Here again the area was dotted with tents. Trail Camp is the most popular campsite for hikers who like to take a few days to climb the peak; it's probably the sanest choice for recuperating and acclimating to the elements before tackling the next stage: the infamous stretch of ninety-seven switchbacks that loomed beyond the camp and disappeared into the horizon. Hikers have often claimed this as the hardest and most monotonous segment of the hike. I soon found out they were correct; total exhaustion set in soon after the climb. I stepped aside to let a group pass.

"How's it going?" a hiker asked.

"Great! After all, I'm only seventy years old." As I was close to giving up, I meant my remark as pure sarcasm. The hikers looked at each other.

"Seventy?" one remarked. Then a round of applause followed.

The last hiker in the group noticed the pouch around my waist and remarked, "Doing it in a day, are you?"

"Yeah, stupid, huh?"

"Well, it takes a stud to do that!"

As a member of the Viagra generation, being called a stud was undoubtedly the greatest compliment any man could receive. It was with this encouragement I continued the trek, taking it one step at a time.

A little farther on, a large icy patch appeared on the trail. On the other side was an intimidating rock cliff descending hundreds of feet below. Totally unprepared for this situation, both physically and mentally, this felt like a great excuse to retreat.

"Don't worry, this mountain ain't going nowhere," commented a hiker who was taking a rest and chewing on a candy bar nearby.

I agreed with him wholeheartedly, but then, as an afterthought, I told myself, *Yeah, but my days are numbered.* Nevertheless, I turned around and headed back to my car.

The following week, I felt ready to make a second attempt to climb Whitney, and this time I was better prepared. I slept a little longer the night before (I parked in a secluded corner of the lot, where other hikers wouldn't disturb me), and had a less powerful but longer lasting flashlight, warm gloves, and crampons for walking over icy terrain. The weather was warm and started out absolutely calm and perfect, with not a speck of cloud in the sky, but by midmorning, the wind had picked up and the temperature plunged below zero. I was not prepared for that. By the time I made it to Trail Camp, I was shivering so much I could barely walk. I was afraid hypothermia would set in if I kept going, so calling off the hike was the only sane thing to do. Even my attempt to derive energy from a PowerBar was unsuccessful, since my dentures couldn't make a dent in the frozen snack.

The following week, the snow level was down to eight thousand feet, and it appeared that the trail would be closed until the following spring. It was another excellent excuse for returning home. Still lacking the confidence to make it to the summit, it was indeed a relief to have a legitimate excuse for postponing the event.

Another year passed, and remembering the encouragement from other hikers I met on other trails, I made preparations for my third attempt at Whitney.

"I feel kind of tired today. There is always tomorrow, and the mountain isn't going anywhere." I often said this sort of thing when I wanted to scrap a hike and return to the comfort of my truck. Finally, however, I realized it was often sheer determination that could take a hiker to the summit. And so I pressed on. There were times when I had to stop for a rest every hundred feet, but instead of giving up, I just waited a while for my second wind to kick in, and in that way I was able to make it to the top of many impressive peaks. I simply kept repeating, "I'll go another one hundred feet, I'll go another one hundred feet" with each step I took.

One pint of energy drink and one pint of water plus a

Slim-Fast bar and two Essentials energy bars were all the food and drink I had with me on this third attempt at the Big One. Inside my waist pouch were a Gortex jacket, a hood, iodine water treatment pills, a spare flashlight, spare batteries, denture adhesive, Pepto Bismol, a first aid kit, and two small sealable plastic bags for bringing back used toilet paper, in accordance with the slogan "Pack it in, pack it out." Since I was partial to traveling light, this compact pouch and its contents seemed to suit my needs. Attached to my belt were small crampons, a camera, gloves, a small Swiss Army knife, a thermometer, a compass, and a headlamp. In my pants pockets were a topographic map and a pen as well as some more batteries.

Again, departing after work on Friday evening, I arrived at Whitney Portal around 11 p.m. but didn't fall asleep until past 1 a.m. Nevertheless, I was on Mount Whitney Trail by 4:15. I was amazed at what a difference the additional year of conditioning had made; the hike to Trail Camp seemed a lot easier, and I was there in no time.

After completing the ninety-seven switchbacks from Trail Camp—almost two hours of zigzagging later—I arrived at Trail Crest, about eighteen hundred feet higher. The scenery over the crest onto the other side of the mountain was just awesome and reminded me of a scene from the old movie *Lost Horizon*, the story of lost men who crossed a mountain into a secluded valley where people lived peacefully forever.

Up at the crest, near fourteen thousand feet, I felt the impact of the thinner air. This segment of the Whitney climb is thought to be the point at which hikers are the most vulnerable to altitude sickness. I began to feel a bit woozy myself but continued on.

The last leg—finally!—was from Trail Crest to the summit, a distance of slightly over two miles with an elevation gain of seven hundred feet. This part of the trail was devoid of vegetation, and the only signs of life were the marmots. Yet it was spectacular in its own way; I could still see the breathtaking view into lush King's Canyon and Sequoia National Park on the west side of the Sierra Nevada Range.

This final sector was steep and rocky, with only a faint trail to the summit. When the stone cabin that marked the top appeared to me over the terrain, I raised my hands to the air in triumph and joy.

In front of the cabin was a flat metal registration box with columns marked Date, Name, City, State, and Comments.

I learned later that the cabin was built of flat stones from the surrounding area, and the mortar, lumber, and other building materials had been transported up the narrow trail by donkeys. The structure was built by the Smithsonian Institution in 1909 as an astronomical outpost and was equipped with a sixteen-inch telescope to study life on Mars, which at the time was a logical scientific venture.

On the door was a sign warning of lightning hazard.

I wasn't alone at the summit, and another hiker directed my attention to the half dozen metal rods sticking up from the cabin roof, installed to channel electricity into the ground rather than taking an express path through some unfortunate mortal standing on this, the highest point in the contiguous forty-eight states.

As I looked around, I kept saying to myself, "I can't believe it. This can't be true. I'm on the summit of Mount Whitney. Is this just an illusion?"

I had only been on the trail for six hours and fifty-four minutes.

"Hank! You made it!" I heard two familiar voices in the distance. It was Dorothy and Dave, a complete surprise! I never imagined I'd meet someone I knew at the summit. Dorothy gave me a hug, as elated as I was that I had finally made a successful trek up Mount Whitney.

As I lay on the flat, sandy ground, I was overcome with gratification as well as a feeling that I was living in a world of fantasy. It was difficult to believe I was there at the top of the Big One at the age of seventy-one, a full fifty-seven years after I had made a vow from behind the barbed wire fence to climb Mount Whitney when I became a free man. I made ten more treks to the Whitney summit after that, and each time I was filled with the same exhilaration.

"The cloud's coming in," I overheard one hiker tell his friends. They began to prepare for a descent to their tents at a lower camp.

I felt the cold front sweeping over the summit and, not ready to go down yet, sought shelter in the stone cabin. The hinge on the door was broken, and there was evidence it had been a forced entry, perhaps by some desperate hiker seeking refuge. I joined half a dozen other hikers who were already inside and sat on the wooden floor and leaned against the wall.

Thump! We heard a noise coming from under the wooden floor.

"Marmot. They're taking shelter under the cabin," another hiker assured us when he saw our bewildered expressions.

Through the open door, we could see the wind carrying snowflakes and rain droplets across the summit. It was neither a rainstorm nor a snowstorm, but whatever it was was enough to keep me sitting in the comfort of the cabin, even as other hikers departed one by one, leaving me the only remaining person at the summit of Mount Whitney.

It's only four o'clock, I thought. *I'll wait another hour before taking off.* It turned out to be a good decision, since an hour later the storm had subsided and the sky was again clear.

When I arrived at the switchback section on the return trek, I was surprised to see that Trail Camp below was covered with fresh snow. Apparently, the summit—at 14,500 feet—had been above the clouds, but at the camp a few thousand feet below, it had snowed enough to cover almost all the landmarks, the one major exception being the black outhouse. When I arrived at the camp, it was dark and deserted, and it was only then that I became aware of the severity of the snowstorm. The trail was completely covered with snow, and with no footprints or landmarks to guide me, I was totally disoriented. I knew the trail passed by the outhouse, but beyond that, it was a hit-or-miss situation. I walked past the outhouse and kept going until it was almost out of sight (which was not far, since it was already dark). Not knowing where to go from there, and still not recognizing my surroundings, I trudged my way back to the outhouse and started off in another direction.

"Oomph!" Out of nowhere, I fell into a cavity between two boulders camouflaged with snow. It was soft snow, and I could hear it making a slushing sound as it packed against my legs up to my crotch. I couldn't budge my legs, so the only thing to do was dig out with my hands. In the next little while, I fell into two more cavities, and the more I fell and dug out, fell and dug out, the more I could feel my feet and hands becoming numb. Never sure I had found the right trail, I trudged back to the outhouse time and again before venturing into another direction.

Finally, a couple of footprints! With the joy of salvation, I followed the tracks until I realized they were going down a slope that didn't resemble any stretch on the Whitney trail. As I stopped to reorient myself again, I noticed two hikers at the bottom of a ravine wandering around in circles with their flashlights.

They must be lost, too, I thought. Since they were out of yelling range, I did not attempt to contact them and instead returned to the outhouse. I figured as long as the outhouse was in sight, and as long as I kept walking, I didn't have anything to fear. The one thing I couldn't do was stop to rest, since that would put me at risk of hypothermia, and I didn't want to end up a frozen chunk of meat. I had to keep walking through the night and on until sunrise, when hikers would be arriving, leaving their footprints in the snow.

I looked at my wristwatch. It was 1:30 in the morning. I had been wandering in the snow for more than six hours. I began to wonder if I could last until sunrise since my extremities were becoming numb in spite of my constant motion. All the excitement and elation of having finally summited Whitney was now replaced with fear and uncertainty.

Suddenly, I heard faint voices in the darkness. Were they coming from a nearby tent? I stopped and listened, then slowly walked in the direction of the voices until I saw a faint silhouette of a group of hikers. I didn't know where they had come from—they hadn't been at the summit—but I didn't care because at least now I had company. It didn't even matter that they were also lost. Now I was in a group of six instead of all alone.

After thirty minutes of exploration, one hiker finally shouted out, "Hey, I found the trail!"

I joined the group on the trip down, but not before uttering my gratitude to the black outhouse, the lonely beacon that had kept me safe through the dark, frigid night.

* * *

The following summer, my children—the youngest at thirty-five and the oldest at forty-two—joined me on an ascent to Mount Whitney's summit. I had honored the promise I'd made to my children so many years ago.

Chapter Twelve

CLOSURE

When I arrived at Manzanar, I was an angry and frustrated teenager. I yelled profanity and made disrespectful gestures at the MPs. I was full of aggression and rage. Soon, however, those feelings began to wane, in part because there were plenty of upsides to being a young person in camp, beginning from the moment we arrived.

The construction crew who tarpapered the barracks left behind dozens of circular pieces of tarpaper, which had been used to protect the ends of the rolls in transport. A group of us kids decided to toss them around in the open space of the firebreak. Most of the discs took nosedives, but a few soared overhead, hovered for a moment, picked up speed, and then crashed into nearby barracks with loud thuds that gave us a tremendous rush. Years later, a couple of entrepreneurs made a similar circular piece out of colorful plastic and called it a Frisbee. I still think we had the idea first. The Issei often lectured the younger generation that the United States was a land of opportunity, the very reason they had immigrated to this country in the first place; I don't recall them ever saying we should just stand idly and let chances for success just swoosh on by.

There were also amenities at camp that we didn't have at home. Instead of the usual fly- and spider-infested outhouses and the accompanying stench that seemed to cling to our clothes forever, at Manzanar we had sophisticated plumbing technology, with flushing toilets. We had real toilet paper instead of pages from newspapers and comic books.

Manzanar was an internment camp locked behind barbed wire fences, but it was also a bustling community in which the residents were able to live a somewhat normal life. The young participated in games and sports (and occasional wayward activities) while the mature residents indulged in *shogi* (a Japanese chess game) and traditional Japanese music, and built extravagant gardens and koi ponds to pass their time away.

At the time of our evacuation from the West Coast, the median age of Nisei was seventeen, and the Issei, mostly in their fifties and sixties, were the kingpins of Japanese American culture. The Issei were our role models, and they lived by the phrase *Shikata-ga-nai*, which means "Whatever will be will be. There is one thing we can do, and that is to make the best of what we have at the moment." They said "*Shikata-ga-nai*" as they peacefully led us into the wartime internment camps, where they spent the next several years patiently waiting for better days to come. And when the war was over, they continued on with their lives, picking up where they had left off. This was the legacy they gave us, and it's a legacy to make their children and grandchildren proud of their Japanese ancestry.

After the war ended and the camp residents had relocated across the country and around the world, Manzanar was disassembled. The lease on the land, owned by Los Angeles Department of Water and Power, was terminated and many barracks were either sold to local residents or dismantled and used for other purposes. The plumbing and wiring was auctioned off as well. The razing of what was left began in 1946, with bulldozers burying the gardens and ponds and leveling everything in between, leaving only the concrete slabs of former warehouses, latrines, laundry and ironing rooms, and the hundreds of water faucets that had stood at the corner of each barrack. The only building left untouched was the high school auditorium.

Since the closure of Manzanar, I had passed by the dilapidated green structure on Highway 395 many times, but it wasn't until 1985 that I drove into the camp area, my former home. There were gullies cutting across the old asphalt roads and meandering through the one-square-mile area that had once been a dynamic wartime community. From the highway, it looked like just another wasteland spotted with small groves of black locusts and cottonwood trees among the lush blue-gray sagebrush terrain.

Forty years later, the water faucets were still dotting the landscape, although all but one were missing their upper sections, where the scallop-shaped handles had been. The one faucet, among hundreds, that had remained mostly intact had a damaged handle that someone had crudely repaired with a piece of wood and a length of rusty wire, forming a makeshift bandage. *That's the only pipe left in the entire camp that shows what the faucet with a handle actually looked like!* I thought. It was a small detail but a huge memento of the three years and three months I had spent at Manzanar. This one-of-a-kind remnant of our camp was a part of my history—of *our* history—and I didn't like the idea of it being left in the desert sun to rust and eventually disappear. I resolved to dig it out and take it with me. The only tool I had with me was a pair of pliers, and I couldn't get the one-inch pipe to even budge.

I was so excited about the artifact that I returned to Manzanar the following Saturday with a twelve-inch and a fifteen-inch pipe wrench, but the pipe, buried two feet deep, seemed to be permanently fused in place. It was a futile attempt.

Undaunted, a week later I made a third 250-mile trek back to Manzanar, this time with a fifteen-inch pipe wrench fitted with a three-foot extension for extra leverage. The adrenaline really kicked in when I heard a faint snapping noise as the pipe loosened its grip from beneath the surface of the desert. This pipe, a keepsake from Manzanar, instantly became one of my prized possessions, and for the next nineteen years, it rested safe and sound in my garage.

When Manzanar became a historic site in 1992 and the old auditorium was renovated to become an interpretive center open to the public in 2004, I sent the pipe back to Manzanar and in return received a letter of appreciation for the donation. Proud of my deed, I showed the letter to my children, expecting they would share my enthusiasm.

"How come they sent you a thank-you letter?" Karen asked with a frown on her face. "You stole the pipe, Dad, and all you did was return it to the rightful owner."

She was right. Realizing that I was indeed a thief, I decided to come clean and return the other artifacts I had stolen from the site, including several coins I had found with my metal detector in the area of the former outdoor movie theater, and also the clothesline post I'd uncovered at Block 17, where the people from Venice, California, had once lived.

As for the three beautiful boulders I'd stolen from the waterfall garden in Block 9, they are permanently cemented into a small rock garden and pond in my backyard. At this moment, I have no immediate plans to disassemble the structure, and I'm hopeful a sincere public apology to the Terminal Islanders who once lived in that block will suffice.

* * *

In January 1993, I received the following letter regarding the government's attempt to make amends to former internees in the form of a redress payment of $20,000 each:

U.S. Department of Justice
Civil Rights Division
Office of Redress Administration
Office of the Administrator
Washington, D.C.

January 28, 1993

Dear Correspondent:

The Office of Redress Administration (ORA) is interested in expediting the processing of your redress case. ORA has sought to contact you several times in the past in order to obtain the necessary documentation to verify your case for payment. It is imperative that you provide ORA with the documents that we have previously requested. As of this date, however, you have not responded to our requests.

Accordingly, if you want your case reviewed for payment, you must immediately forward the proof documents previously requested by ORA. However, if you do not respond to ORA within fifteen business days from the receipt of this letter, we will conclude that you wish to have your case closed. In other words, your case will not be reviewed for payment.

If the person to whom this correspondence is addressed is deceased, please call ORA for further instructions. Inquiries may also be made by writing ORA. If you have additional questions or require assistance, please contact ORA.

Again, if we do not receive the requested information from you within the next fifteen business days, we will consider your case closed. Thank you for your prompt attention to this matter.

Sincerely,
Paul W. Suddes (Signed)
Administrator for Redress

Let it be clear that I have great respect and admiration for Sue Embrey, of the Manzanar Committee, and for the hundreds of others who diligently contributed their time to the redress effort, which brought the violation of our civil rights into public awareness. Their efforts have resulted in the preservation of former camps, including Manzanar, and helped discourage similar injustices in the future.

Without doubt, we got screwed big time when we were forcibly confined in relocation camps. There's no denying that fact. And yet I don't want that to be what we are remembered for. I want the Japanese Americans who lived through World War II to be honored in our nation's history as people who peacefully and courageously survived these hardships and humiliation and, after the war, continued on in our lives with dignity and success.

I declined the $20,000 redress money and sent the following letter explaining why:

U.S. Department of Justice
Office of Redress Administration
Washington, D.C.

February 5, 1993

To the United States Department of Justice:

Thank you for your kind concern regarding the redress payment, and I wish to apologize for not responding to your previous letters. Classic today is the account of Issei (Japanese immigrants) and Nisei (second-generation Americans of Japanese ancestry) who left their peaceful communities for Relocation Centers so remote that they weren't even on the map. Manzanar was one of these camps. Describe Manzanar as you will...and you are probably correct. Sand, wind, ice, heat and 36 blocks of tar-papered barracks. But when people came, they planted lawns, trees and shrubs. They dug holes and built ponds, rock gardens, waterfalls and wishing wells. They pooled their cultural resources and started flower arrangement, shuji and shigin classes and dozens more. Competition was fierce, from baseball to gymnastics to judo. The educational system and its requirements were just as high as any other American school. Industry flourished, from furniture production to tofu and even miso manufacturing. Farmers transformed barren desert wasteland into productive farmland. This was the industrial, cultural and agricultural Manzanar...and for a while, it was my home. I claim this former desert community, for it is so much a part of me. Occasionally, when I feel disgusted with the greed, crime and immorality existing within our present society, I return to Owens Valley and what used to be Manzanar; and then I become well and confident again because I am reminded of those diligent Issei and Nisei, who with pride and determination faced that wartime episode as just another interlude in one's life...and ventured into totally unfamiliar and often hostile communities to start their lives from "square one."

I am enclosing a photograph of Manzanar Park (circa 1944) with the pond, bridge and garden with the barracks in the background. I was only in my teens at the time...too young to contribute to many of these aesthetic projects, but whenever I look at this picture, I cannot help but to admire and respect those older folks who created such beauty and serenity in the midst of the inequality, bigotry, hatred and injustice which surrounded our everyday life.

I am hereby declining the redress payment because: Instead of being considered a victim of injustice, I would rather have the Japanese Americans go down in history as a patient, proud and courageous group who endured that wartime incident peacefully with pride, courage and determination, and I hope that someday there will be peace all around us and that all mankind can live in harmony without hatred and prejudice forever.

Sincerely,
Hank (Henry) Shozo Umemoto (Signed)

I received a letter shortly thereafter stating: "Your record of written refusal has been filed with ORA and the amount shall remain in the Civil Liberties Public Education Fund."

At the time I mailed my letter, I secretly wished that perhaps hundreds of years in the future some scholar might find my letter in the government's archives and start exposing more of the peaceful and beautiful moments at Manzanar. As fate would have it, my wish started to become a reality, and much sooner than I had anticipated.

In 2006, I became a docent at Manzanar and had the rare opportunity to join an archaeological dig team, led by National Park Service archaeologist Jeff Burton, in excavating the gardens and ponds buried for more than half a century on Manzanar grounds. One dig in particular was filled with suspense and mystery. Jeff got a clue from an old issue of the *Manzanar Free Press*, a camp newspaper, that a garden between Barracks 3 and 4 in Block 16 had won third prize in the camp beautification contest. Jeff located the spot, but when we went to the area, we found it covered with sagebrush and absolutely no evidence of a garden or a pond. We didn't even know exactly what we were looking for. Jeff poked around with a rod for a while and eventually located several stones arranged in a row, which could have been a border for a pond. We followed the trail of stones, exposing adjoining rocks one at a time, and as we progressed, we began to uncover a weird, snaky pattern. It appeared we were looking at a former pond, although one unlike the more conventional kidney-shaped ponds we were familiar with. I remember making a nasty (and regrettable) comment that the guy who built whatever it was must have been high on *shochu*. We continued removing the sandy soil a bucketful at a time, and watched as our discovery slowly began to take form: a scallop-shaped pond perhaps fifteen feet or so in diameter, thigh deep, with an island in the middle. What a find!

This was just one among the many gardens and ponds excavated in recent years, and there are many more still to be discovered. With each excavation, we are reaffirming the resilience of Manzanar's residents—people who turned their prison into a productive community, where they worked and played and patiently dreamt of better days to come amid the serenity and beauty of gardens and ponds with cascading waterfalls and carp whirling in the waters under black locust trees.

* * *

In 2011, I received a $25,000 grant from the California State Library to publish this book. It came to my attention sometime after receiving the grant that the money was part of the Civil Liberties Public Education Program, which was where my declined $20,000 redress check had been deposited back in 1993. Whether it is a coincidence or a miracle, the thought makes me smile in bewilderment. In any case, I am deeply grateful.

More than 115,000 men, women, and children were affected by Executive Order 9066, leaving each with a unique and remarkable tale. My chronicle is just one among the 120,000 stories, almost all of which are now buried in the sands of time forever.

Acknowledgements

Just for the heck of it, during the late 1980s I wrote a series of three-hundred-word personal essays—one a month for forty-eight consecutive months—and sent them to my children. A few stories were published in the *Rafu Shimpo* newspaper and the *Nanka Nikkei Voices Journal*, and some of those who read the stories commented on how surprised they were since I don't look or talk like the intellectual type. My sincere thanks go to these people, who in their way encouraged me to continue my writing endeavors.

Those forty-eight stories were laid to rest for the next twenty years, until 2011, when I accidentally stumbled onto the files and, just for the heck of it, printed and bound the stories for my children. When my daughter Karen and son-in-law Brian asked if I minded if they tried to get the collection published, my reply was simply, "Do whatever you want with it." To Karen and Brian, then, go my thanks for putting this project into motion by contacting my publisher and obtaining my grant and following through with contributing to every aspect of the project to the very end.

When Malcolm Margolin, publisher at Heyday, was contacted, he commented that I lacked professionalism but had a bizarre sense of humor and a unique writing talent that, although amateurish, was enough to commit him to publishing the stories. My appreciation goes to Malcolm for plunking down his bet on a longshot.

With Malcolm and Heyday attached to the project, the California State Library issued a grant to see it through. To the California State Library and the California Civil Liberties Public Education Program, I wish to express my gratitude.

To best present the manuscript in a professional manner, I sought the aid of Naomi Hirahara, an educator and seasoned author of several books pertaining to Japanese American culture. She suggested the title *Manzanar to Mount Whitney* and introduced the concept of weaving my internment camp stories into my hiking narratives. I thank Naomi for making this volume unique—different than any other book ever published on the topic.

To further refine the text, Gayle Wattawa and Lisa K. Marietta of Heyday pored over the manuscript and made numerous helpful comments and suggestions. I am indebted to Gayle and Lisa for their expertise in transforming a group of random stories into a captivating, cohesive book.

Without the encouragement and support of all these people along the way, the stories I had written "just for the heck of it" might have remained in my computer, archived among the dead files, until they were eventually deleted, forever forgotten.

About the Author

Hank Umemoto was born in 1928 to immigrant grape farmers in Florin, a rural community near Sacramento, California. At the age of thirteen, he and his family—along with 115,000 men, women, and children of Japanese ancestry—were evacuated from the West Coast and imprisoned by the U.S. government in internment camps for the duration of World War II.

Hank spent three years and three months at Manzanar War Relocation Center, located in the eastern foothills of the Sierra Nevada Range. From inside the five-strand barbed wire enclosure on the desert floor, he often gazed at the zigzagging Whitney Portal Road that led to the main trail going up Mount Whitney, the highest peak in the contiguous United States. He always dreamt of climbing the Big One someday.

After his release from camp, he moved to Los Angeles, where he spent the first three and a half years living in skid row. After finishing high school, he worked to support himself and his mother while attending Los Angeles City College. During the Korean War, he served overseas in the army with 38th Military Intelligence Service. After his discharge, he attended Cal State Los Angeles using funds from the GI Bill, then married, raised a family, and worked in a variety of trades and businesses. His jobs included gardener, owner of a jewelry store, owner of a mail-order business, and insurance agent with Cal Western Life. He eventually started a print shop and remained in the printing business for thirty-two years, until his retirement in his mid-seventies. He now writes for enjoyment during his sunset years.

HEYDAY

into California

About Heyday

Heyday is an independent, nonprofit publisher and unique cultural institution. We promote widespread awareness and celebration of California's many cultures, landscapes, and boundary-breaking ideas. Through our well-crafted books, public events, and innovative outreach programs we are building a vibrant community of readers, writers, and thinkers.

Thank You

It takes the collective effort of many to create a thriving literary culture. We are thankful to all the thoughtful people we have the privilege to engage with. Cheers to our writers, artists, editors, storytellers, designers, printers, bookstores, critics, cultural organizations, readers, and book lovers everywhere!

We are especially grateful for the generous funding we've received for our publications and programs during the past year from foundations and hundreds of individual donors. Major supporters include:

Acorn Naturalists; Alliance for California Traditional Artists; Anonymous; James J. Baechle; Bay Tree Fund; S. D. Bechtel, Jr. Foundation; Barbara Jean and Fred Berensmeier; Berkeley Civic Arts Program and Civic Arts Commission; Joan Berman; Buena Vista Rancheria; Lewis and Sheana Butler; California Civil Liberties Public Education Program, California State Library; California Council for the Humanities; The Keith Campbell Foundation; Center for California Studies; Jon Christensen; The Christensen Fund; Compton Foundation; Lawrence Crooks; Nik Dehejia; Frances Dinkelspiel and Gary Wayne; Troy Duster; Euclid Fund at the East Bay Community Foundation; Mark and Tracy Ferron; Judith Flanders; Karyn and Geoffrey Flynn; Furthur Foundation; The Fred Gellert Family Foundation; Wallace Alexander Gerbode Foundation;

Nicola W. Gordon; Wanda Lee Graves and Stephen Duscha; Alice Guild; Walter & Elise Haas Fund; Coke and James Hallowell; Hawaii Sons, Inc.; Sandra and Charles Hobson; G. Scott Hong Charitable Trust; Humboldt Area Foundation; The James Irvine Foundation; Kendeda Fund; Marty and Pamela Krasney; Kathy Kwan and Robert Eustace; Guy Lampard and Suzanne Badenhoop; LEF Foundation; Judith and Brad Lowry-Croul; Kermit Lynch Wine Merchant; Michael McCone; Michael Mitrani; Michael J. Moratto, in memory of Ernest L. Cassel; National Wildlife Federation; Steven Nightingale; Pacific Legacy, Inc.; Patagonia, Inc.; John and Frances Raeside; Redwoods Abbey; Robin Ridder; Alan Rosenus; The San Francisco Foundation; San Manuel Band of Mission Indians; Sonoma Land Trust; Martha Stanley; Roselyne Chroman Swig; Thendara Foundation; Sedge Thomson and Sylvia Brownrigg; Tides Foundation; TomKat Charitable Trust; The Roger J. and Madeleine Traynor Foundation; Marion Weber; White Pine Press; John Wiley & Sons, Inc.; The Dean Witter Foundation; Lisa Van Cleef and Mark Gunson; Bobby Winston; and Yocha Dehe Wintun Nation.

Board of Directors

Getting Involved

To learn more about our publications, events, membership club, and other ways you can participate, please visit www.heydaybooks.com.

Related Titles

For other Japanese American titles, please visit www.heydaybooks.com.

Children of Manzanar
Edited by Heather C. Lindquist

An intimate photographic remembrance of incarceration through the eyes of children, *Children of Manzanar* captures the experiences of the nearly four thousand children and young adults held at Manzanar during World War II.

"[An] extraordinary collection of photographs and personal recollections" —*School Library Journal*, starred review

Copublished with the Manzanar History Association

Journey to Topaz
Yoshiko Uchida

In a bleak and dusty prison camp, eleven-year-old Yuki and her family experience both true friendship and heart-wrenching tragedy. *Journey to Topaz* explores the consequences of prejudice and the capacities of the human spirit. First published in 1971, this book is now a much loved and widely read classic.

*Making Home from War: Stories of Japanese
American Exile and Resettlement*
Edited by Brian Komei Dempster

Written by twelve Japanese American elders who gathered regularly at the Japanese Cultural and Community Center of Northern California, *Making Home from War* is a collection of stories about their exodus from concentration camps into a world that in a few short years had drastically changed.

*Only What We Could Carry: The Japanese
American Internment Experience*
Edited with an Introduction by Lawson Fusao Inada;
Preface by Patricia Wakida; Afterword by William Hohri

Through personal documents, art, and propaganda, *Only What We Could Carry* expresses the fear, confusion and anger of the camp experience. The only anthology of its kind, it is an emotional and intellectual testament to the dignity, spirit and strength of the Japanese American internees.

"It conveys the deep anguish felt by Japanese who defined themselves as citizens of the United States and yet lost their rights as citizens during a time of national fear."—*School Library Journal*

A project of the California Civil Liberties Public Education Program

Printed in the USA
CPSIA information can be obtained
at www.ICGtesting.com
JSHW022333140824
68134JS00019B/1458